Breaking Through:

Building a World-Class Wealth Management Business

Second Edition

John J. Bowen Jr.
Paul Brunswick
Jonathan J. Powell

Breaking Through: Building a World-Class Wealth Management Business
By John J. Bowen Jr., Paul Brunswick and Jonathan Powell

© Copyright 2013 CEG Worldwide, LLC. All rights reserved.

No part of this publication may be reproduced or retransmitted in any form or by any means, including, but not limited to, electronic, mechanical, photocopying, recording or any information storage retrieval system, without the prior written permission of the publisher. Unauthorized copying may subject violators to criminal penalties as well as liabilities for substantial monetary damages up to $100,000 per infringement, costs and attorneys' fees.

The information contained herein is accurate to the best of the publisher's knowledge; however, the publisher can accept no responsibility for the accuracy or completeness of such information or for loss or damage caused by any use thereof.

CEG Worldwide, LLC • 1954 Hayes Lane • San Martin, CA 95046 • (888) 551-3824
www.cegworldwide.com • info@cegworldwide.com

Table of Contents

INTRODUCTION TO THE SECOND EDITION 3

CHAPTER 1: Your Future Success 7

CHAPTER 2: Bridging the Knowing-Doing Gap 15

CHAPTER 3: Attract Affluent Clients 25

CHAPTER 4: Strengthen Client Relationships 53

CHAPTER 5: Capture Assets and Acquire Clients 93

CHAPTER 6: Manage Your Practice as a Business 115

CHAPTER 7: Partner with Institutions and Other Professionals 139

CHAPTER 8: Commit to Lifelong Learning 159

CHAPTER 9: Build Maximum Equity 171

CHAPTER 10: Making It Real 179

ABOUT THE AUTHORS 185

This book is dedicated to all who made it possible:

Our corporate and coaching clients,

who taught us what truly works in our industry

Our teammates at CEG Worldwide,

who brought it all together

And our families,

who make it all worthwhile

Introduction to the Second Edition

WHEN WE WROTE THE FIRST EDITION OF THIS BOOK IN late 2007, the Great Recession was still ahead of us. While the housing bubble had burst and there were ominous economic signs on the horizon, the U.S. stock market had reached all-time highs and few could have predicted the depth of the crisis that was to come.

Now as we write this second edition in 2013, we appear to be—at least for the most part—on the other side of that crisis. Nonetheless, the past five years have left a stamp of uncertainty and apprehension that has perhaps not been seen since the Depression years of the 1930s. Virtually no one—including the most experienced investors and financial advisors—has not had their confidence shaken.

Our primary intent in writing this second edition is to revisit the main theme of the first. In that earlier edition, we asserted that there were tremendous opportunities available for financial advisors who attracted the right clients and served them extremely well. To capture those opportunities, we said, financial advisors must act deliberately, designing their businesses to provide comprehensive wealth management for the affluent while employing proven strategies to grow their assets and net income. In short, they had to be successful on purpose.

Against the new backdrop of uncertainty, some may wonder if the old rules still hold true. Do the same types of opportunities still exist? Are affluent clients looking for a different experience? Should financial advisors take some other approach?

For us, the answers are clear: Not only have the old rules withstood the tests of economic crisis, they are more valid than ever. In fact, both in our work with today's elite financial advisors and in our recent industry research, we see greater opportunity for financial advisors than we have ever seen before.

In the current environment, successful individuals and families are hungry for trusted guidance that helps them achieve their most important financial goals and dreams. Every day, we see that the financial advisors who step up to fill that role and provide that leadership are experiencing unprecedented levels of success. Our goal is to help you do the same—to do very well by your clients and, as a result, do very well for yourself.

Throughout this second edition, we have updated much of our previous research with data drawn from studies conducted over the past several years. We have also incorporated a large number of enhancements to the best practices and strategies we recommend—refinements that are drawn directly from our daily work with many of the nation's top financial advisors.

Over the past five years, we have made it a priority to take advantage of new technologies in video recording in order to make our research and recommendations more accessible to more people. As a result, you will find numerous links to online video resources throughout this book. Perusing these resources will give you a deeper and richer understanding of our strategies than we could ever provide in an old-fashioned book made out of paper. We invite you to explore them fully.

Finally, we have scattered throughout this book links to video profiles of some of our best friends and coaching clients—financial advisors who have built hugely rewarding businesses by providing world-class wealth management to their affluent clients.

We wish you the best of success as you move forward in building the practice of your dreams.

Chapter 1
Your Future Success

WHAT A FABULOUS INDUSTRY WE'RE IN. AS A FINANCIAL advisor, you have opportunities before you that are greater today than ever before. In light of this extraordinary potential, we have written this book to provide you with a clear road map for achieving your greatest possible success and creating a business that's everything you have always hoped it would be.

Let's set some context. According to the most recent data, the United States—the world's wealthiest nation and the undisputed leader of free-market capitalism—has 313.9 million people and 114.7 million households. Of those households, just over three million have more than $1 million in investable assets.

Every major study that we have conducted here at CEG Worldwide, a leading coaching firm for elite financial advisors, shows that more than 90 percent of these affluent individuals want to work with a top financial advisor—if only they can find the right one. If that's the case, why are so many financial advisors not achieving everything they want? Why are so many stuck at the same income level, with the same business model and the same clients? Why aren't more financial advisors moving swiftly toward the success that they know can be theirs?

Finding the answers to these questions—and then sharing those answers with financial advisors—is the journey that the three authors of this book have been on their entire careers. Together, we have nearly 90 years of industry experience, serving as financial advisors, corporate executives and now as partners in CEG Worldwide.

We also have three other things of great value to share with you:

- An extraordinary depth of empirical research—real facts and figures—about how our industry is changing and about what works and what doesn't work

- Proven strategies for success—strategies that are replicable, reliable and road-tested by the hundreds of financial advisors we have worked with in our coaching programs

- A commitment to sharing what we've learned so that you can achieve major breakthroughs and transform your practice into the business you have always wanted

What does it mean to create a breakthrough? We are not interested in incremental steps toward the next level. We want you to set goals that inspire awe—in yourself and in everyone around you—and to perform at a substantially higher level than you ever thought possible. We urge you to pull out all the stops to see where your business can really take you and your clients.

Being Successful on Purpose: Doing What Works

There are approximately 587,000 registered financial advisors in the United States. About 472,000 of them work with individuals. If these 472,000 financial advisors are chasing three million wealthy households—those with more than $1 million in investable assets—then simple math shows that there are fewer than seven such wealthy households per advisor. Significantly growing your income in this competitive environment is challenging, and many financial advisors are dissatisfied with their incomes. In fact, in a survey of more than 2,100 financial advisors that we conducted in 2012, a mere 5.5 percent reported being very satisfied with their incomes. Just 12.7 percent were very satisfied with the growth of their practices.

However, many of the financial advisors who've been through CEG Worldwide's coaching programs have been able to significantly grow their incomes as they transform their practices. Why are these advisors able to vault their productivity, build great businesses, do a great job for their clients and enjoy the quality of life that they want—while so many other advisors never seem to go anywhere? We wrote this book to answer these questions and to give you seven specific strategies that will jump-start you on your own path to success.

But before you start down that road, there's a simple philosophy you must embrace: If you want to succeed, you must be successful on purpose. You are unlikely to haphazardly stumble into great success. Instead, you need a deliberate, focused approach to forging a highly profitable business that serves your clients well and provides you with the lifestyle you want.

We define "success on purpose" this way:

- **Vision:** Knowing exactly where you want to go, what type of business you want to build and whom you want to serve.

- **Focus:** Focusing your activities only on those that bring you closer to achieving your goals.

- **Deliberation:** Moving thoughtfully as you prioritize actions, articulate your plans and hold yourself accountable to your plans.

- **Confidence:** Knowing that, because you are providing your clients a world-class experience that adds significant value to their lives, you do not hesitate to speak out clearly about your offering.

- **Collaboration:** Enlisting others to help you. This includes not only your internal team, but also strategic partners, industry experts and even your top clients.

- **Consistency:** Doing things at the same high level in the same way all the time in order to ensure a top-quality, replicable client experience and build equity in your practice.

Ironically, most financial advisors are already successful with the investment side of their businesses. Yes, we might debate the fine points of exactly how often to rebalance a portfolio or whether one should favor international over domestic funds at a particular point in time. However, so much academic research has been done on investment methodology and asset allocation that most advisors are doing a sound job with their clients' investments. We might argue about the last 5 percent of how to manage our clients' money, but 95 percent of the solution is clearly visible and available to any advisor willing to use it.

But when it comes to how financial advisors manage their practices, things are quite different. Most advisors approach their businesses in a kind of entrepreneurial fog, caught up in the day-to-day necessities of making a living and without a clear direction. Some firms provide advisors with ongoing training opportunities, but for the most part these are product-centric or technically oriented. Little thought is generally given to practice management and business development.

To fill this gap, CEG Worldwide has taken the rigors of empirical research used so successfully on the investment side and applied them to the best practices of top financial advisors. We've studied thousands of financial advisors and affluent clients and have identified the best practices of the leading advisors in the industry—those who consistently earn the top incomes. We've taken this knowledge and distilled it into seven key strategies. These strategies—which form the basis for our in-depth coaching program—have enabled many advisors to be successful on purpose and build the practices and lifestyles they have always wanted. Now we're sharing them with you.

An Overview of the Seven Strategies

Based on extensive industry research and our experience in working with hundreds of financial advisors in our coaching programs and thousands of advisors throughout our combined careers, we have found that the most successful advisors regularly rely on seven key strategies. In fact, it would be fair to say that in nearly every business decision that they're making, these top advisors work toward mastering these seven strategies. Each of these strategies is further composed of a number of specific tactics, many of which we will discuss in detail in this book. As you read through the seven strategies, ask yourself how many of them you already follow. For those that you haven't already fully adopted, consider whether they make sense to you on a gut level.

Strategy One: Attract Affluent Private Clients

In many ways life—and career success—is a numbers game. To succeed on purpose as a financial advisor, you simply must work with fewer, more-affluent clients. Leveraging our in-depth research and coaching experience, we will first teach you what you need to know about the affluent. Then we will show you how to focus your business—and create a more desirable quality of life for yourself—by identifying and targeting a specific market niche. We'll share a wealth of tactics for attracting the affluent, such as interviewing centers of influence (COIs) in your niche and making use of pull marketing techniques. With fewer, wealthier clients you will build closer client relationships and deliver far better service. As a result, you'll be given more assets to manage and will generate referrals for additional wealthy clients in your target niche.

Strategy Two: Strengthen Client Relationships

It's sometimes said that people don't care how much you know until they know how much you care. By working very closely with your clients—by implementing the consultative client relationship management approach that we have developed and will spell out for you—you'll show them just how much you care. As you strengthen your client relationships, you'll build the foundation for a wealth management business that will be in alignment both with what your clients want and with what you can profitably provide while achieving the lifestyle you desire.

Strategy Three: Capture Assets and Acquire Clients

Since investments produce the lion's share of most advisors' revenue, we will show you systematic methods both for generating an endless stream of prequalified prospective clients and for capturing more assets from existing clients. For example, you will discover how to capitalize on the fact that 84.6 percent of satisfied affluent clients would be happy to introduce you to qualified prospects. Also, since so many of the very best advisors owe a good deal of their success to referrals from other professional advisors, such as attorneys and accountants, we will home in on exactly how to find and work with these other professionals. Often, it's not even a question of correctly positioning yourself, because the business is already there for the asking. Instead, you just have to know that it's there and how to ask for it. We'll show you how to do both.

Strategy Four: Manage Your Practice as a Business

Consider the great opportunity before you today: Our research found that, on average, financial advisors delivering true wealth management earned net incomes of $881,000 in 2006. We have no reason to believe that wealth managers are any less successful today. Now, you may not have thought that you were signing up to be an entrepreneur when you entered our industry. Nonetheless, we're going to explain why you owe it to all your stakeholders—including your clients—to build not just a good practice and a good job, but also a great and deftly managed business. One important difference between having a great business and having a great job is whether the business is sustainable without you. We will explain how to build a business that can hum along—even grow and expand— even when you're not there.

Strategy Five: Partner with Institutions and Other Professionals

By working well with others, you can accomplish far more than you can on your own. We'll show you how to work with the range of financial institutions and firms that want to partner with you—to their advantage, your advantage and your clients' advantage. In many cases both you and your clients will be better off in the long run if you turn to dedicated specialists to provide many types of investment-related services. We will help you get clear about the tools you most need to best serve your clients, and then we will show you how to find and work with the firms that are aligned with the kind and quality of services you want to provide. You will end up with more time for client-facing activities, and your clients will end up with better service.

Strategy Six: Commit to Lifelong Learning

The biggest asset any of us has is our human capital. We describe how to nurture your own human capital and the human capital of the members of your team. Your reward will be renewed ideas, rekindled enthusiasm and enhanced skill sets. Sometimes those of us who achieve a modicum of success stop attending both personal and industry-relevant workshops and conferences because we feel these are designed for those who are less successful. In truth, as you become more successful it is even more important to be thoughtful about maximizing your human capital in order to continue becoming all that you are capable of being.

Strategy Seven: Realize Maximum Equity

Whether you are an equity stakeholder in your business or an intrapreneur—an employee in an independent firm or in a wirehouse—we will show you how to work toward maximizing your business's value. We will share with you some of the secrets to consistently making smart decisions that will dramatically increase the value of your business. Far too often our businesses become cluttered with nonessential items and processes. But to create maximum value, you need to know how to build a business that runs effortlessly, one that makes your competitors scratch their heads and wonder how you make it all seem so simple. Even if you are never going to sell your business, in the long run each and every one of us will transfer our accounts to others, and therefore it pays to always run your business as if you are planning to sell it for the greatest possible price.

How to Use This Book

As you read through the seven strategies, begin to think of what might be possible if you deployed these strategies. Begin to imagine the ideal business that you might have—the one that gives you the financial success, the benefits for your clients and the personal lifestyle you have always wanted. Don't get caught up in individual strategies or tactics. Instead, give yourself permission to dream big—as big as you can—about your ideal business. Let that dream grow while you read this book. We promise you that the opportunity is out there for you to become as successful as you want. We will show you how to turn that opportunity into reality.

As for how to make all this real, we will discuss that generally throughout the book but specifically in the next chapter and Chapter 10. But for now, we invite you to sit back and relax, open your mind and consider something that we all face: the knowing-doing gap.

Chapter 2
Bridging the Knowing-Doing Gap

MANY OF US BELIEVE WE HAVE TREMENDOUS UNTAPPED potential. We yearn to squeeze all the juice out of our lives and careers but don't know how. Even when we do know how (or think we do), we somehow end up not doing anything about it anyway.

There are two pieces of good news here.

First: You're not alone. Many people, including many successful financial advisors, are frustrated by their inability to move to a higher level of success, even if they think they know what they should do next. But *knowing* what you need to do and actually *doing* it are two very different things. We call this distinction the "knowing-doing gap."

Second: This chapter will explain exactly how to close the knowing-doing gap. Of course, knowing how to do this and actually doing it are two very different things. As Yogi Berra said, "In theory there is no difference between theory and practice. In practice there is."

The Map Is Not the Territory

Where does the knowing-doing gap come from? Consider how we are educated in our culture. For the most part, teachers put forward facts and theories that we study and memorize and we repeat these back during tests. If we pass these tests—especially if we ace them—we think that we really "know" the subject matter and feel pretty good about ourselves.

However, such conceptual learning doesn't give us a very good sense of how to actually do things. For example, you might take a seminar or read some books on turning your practice into a great business. But concept-oriented books and seminars can at best expand and reorient our thinking, and very few people can move directly from better thinking into successful action.

If you have ever been involved in building or remodeling a home or office, you know that there can be a big difference between your conception of the project's outcome and what happens as it is actually built. We think conceptually, but we have to act in the real world, and the real world often doesn't match up with our concepts. As Alfred Korzybski famously said, "The map is not the territory."

This distinction holds for nearly everything you do. For example, you may have an abstract idea of how your first meeting with a client will go, but when you sit down with this particular person, things end up going quite differently. The same thing can hold true as you embark upon building a world-class wealth management practice. Even if you know precisely what your goal is and think you know exactly how to get there, things often work out differently than planned. Like a construction project, things often go wrong, take longer or turn out another way. If you accept this likelihood upfront, you are much more likely to hold steadfast to your plan and succeed in the long run.

Minding the Gaps

Before turning to exactly how to step over the knowing-doing gap, it's important to understand that there are a number of levels within the gap that can impede your progress, as shown in **Exhibit 2.1**.

Advisors at Level 0 are satisfied with things the way things are. Not knowing or caring about Paris, they are content to stay on the farm. As a

EXHIBIT 2.1
Levels of the Knowing-Doing Gap

Level	Type of Gap	Advisor Status	Gap Analysis
4	No gap	Advisor is on his or her way to creating a great business.	All levels of the knowing-doing gap have been successfully overcome.
3	Knowing-doing gap	Advisor starts doing what needs to be done but gets stuck or gives up along the way.	This is the knowing-doing gap proper; it can be overcome by ability to coordinate consistent actions with long-term vision.
2	Commitment gap	Advisor knows what needs to be done but doesn't begin doing it.	There is a lack of motivation, courage or commitment.
1	Knowledge gap	Advisor wants to change but doesn't know how to go forward or has outdated or inaccurate information.	There is a lack of empirical knowledge about what really works and what need to be done.
0	No awareness of gaps	Advisor is satisfied with status quo.	With no desire to change, there is no awareness of any gaps.

Source: CEG Worldwide.

result, they don't contemplate any major changes or new actions. (If you have read this far, then you're beyond this level.)

At Level 1, financial advisors know that much more is possible and are frustrated with their current businesses. They may be good or even exceptional at investing and managing clients' wealth but don't have the entrepreneurial perspective or practice management expertise necessary to move forward. That's where this book and our more in-depth coaching programs become invaluable.

At Level 2, advisors know what needs to be done but don't wholeheartedly step into crafting the necessary plans and taking the required actions. This may be due to a lack of motivation or clarity or a general unwillingness to commit to being successful on purpose. Often, advisors at this level let the unimportant urgent daily grind get in the way of implementing necessary changes. It's critical that these advisors step over this gap by fully committing themselves to making the needed plans and acting in accordance with those plans. At the end of this chapter we'll say more about the rewards that follow from having courage and taking action.

At Level 3, advisors are fully committed to being successful on purpose. Still, because many things can go wrong, or at least differently than planned, many advisors get stuck or give up short of creating the business that they dream of. This is the knowing-doing gap proper and can be overcome with the integral approach to both knowing and doing that we describe next.

Persistent, courageous advisors can overcome this final knowing-doing gap to reach Level 4 and create the profitable world-class businesses and lifestyles they have always dreamed of.

WATCH THE VIDEO ▶ **Profile in Success: Peter Walsh**
Buffalo, New York
www.cegworldwide.com/btbook/peter-walsh

Coordinating Consistent Action and Long-Term Vision

Suppose you read this book, are committed to changing and understand what you need to do to build a great business. Now the hard part begins: stepping out into the real world—the one beyond your conceptual maps—and making it happen. You must convert your knowledge into real-world actions that result in the business you want. Obviously, making all this happen is very different from just talking or thinking about it.

What typically will happen next is that you begin bumping into lots of unexpected barriers. Managers, partners, employees, clients, regulators, and broker-dealers or custodians: No one will behave quite as you expected. Soon enough, you begin thinking, "All that vision stuff is a lot of baloney"—especially when you have to deal with your in-laws, income taxes, office politics and paying the bills. Before long, you are back to reacting to the world as it actually is, and the "knowing" element of your vision is lost.

Combining knowing and doing—putting action and vision together—is a huge challenge for almost everyone. With all the pressures we face, it's very difficult to consistently act in service of our long-term goals. It's almost as if there were a current pushing us away from what we want to achieve.

It will help you stay on course to recognize that there are two domains of knowing and two domains of doing. The result is the four-quadrant Integral Knowing-Doing Grid, as shown in **Exhibit 2.2**.

EXHIBIT 2.2
The Integral Knowing-Doing Grid

	Internal *What do you know*	**External** *What you do*
Individual *Domain of the person*	***Me:*** individual concerns, thoughts, meanings, values and identity ***Field:*** depth psychology	***It:*** individual actions and results; how the individual works ***Field:*** behaviorism
Group *Domain of the group*	***We:*** shared concerns, thoughts, meanings, values, group membership ***Field:*** anthropology	***Its:*** systems, group actions and results, rules and procedures; what firms do ***Field:*** systems research

Source: Ken Wilber, *A Brief History of Everything*, 1996.

The upper-right quadrant is individual action—what you actually do. The upper-left quadrant represents your personal beliefs and thoughts, including who you are as an advisor, the quality of service you want to provide to your clients, and what you want to make of yourself and your business.

The lower-left quadrant is the social sphere. It represents the conversations you have with other industry members and others who influence how you think and help you develop. This includes coaches, your peers, and others in your work and personal life who help you enlarge your thinking. Finally, the lower-right quadrant represents the systems you put into place that enable you to move forward, make things happen and bring your vision into being.

Most of us end up working in just one or two of these quadrants. For example, some of us just take individual actions. We act, act, act, perhaps calling clients, making presentations or selling products. But in all this acting, we end up not learning much about ourselves, we fail to put systems into place and we tend to repeat our mistakes. Likewise, others of us are very good at working on our personal identity, self-image and vision for our futures. We may be really good at writing out our vision statements, but our visions never seem to happen.

To overcome the knowing-doing gap—to get from Level 3 to Level 4—you must tap into each of the quadrants on a regular basis. Find ways to link them up and move from one to another so that they reinforce each other.

For instance, suppose that, as a result of reading this book, you decide to be much more selective about the new clients you take on in the future. You determine the specific market niche you can serve best and most profitably and commit to working only with clients from this niche. This is an action in the external world and so resides in the upper-right quadrant.

To link this with the other quadrants, ask yourself what you are learning from this action and how you feel about it. Then have a conversation about it with one of your colleagues, coaches or loved ones. See how you can incorporate what you learn in this conversation back into your actions as you move forward. Then take another action in the real world. See how that has improved your self-knowledge, next talk to your colleagues about it and then use their feedback to put together an even better system.

Linking the quadrants like this—spiraling out from what you actually do and know to what others think and advise to systems that help you lock it all into place—not only keeps you learning over time, but actually helps you achieve your vision, by encouraging you to take more action and create ever-better systems. You will find it much easier to continue to forge forward when your conceptual plans come up against real-world obstacles. Even in the face of temporary "failures" (perhaps better thought of as "accelerated learning opportunities"), you will be able to continue to coordinate your actions with your long-term vision. And voila! You'll find yourself on the other side of the knowing-doing gap—well on your way to the business of your dreams.

Frustration into Courage, Action into Rewards

We've often found that elite advisors¬—those who succeed in transforming their businesses—are individuals who start out somewhat frustrated. Although their peers and clients see them as successful, they are nonetheless frustrated because they want to create truly great businesses that produce substantially greater incomes, afford a more desirable lifestyle and provide better client service.

So it's okay to be frustrated. It means you are aware that you are missing an opportunity to be and do more. By recognizing and then harnessing that frustration, you will be far more likely to overcome the knowing-doing gap and successfully execute on the strategies we describe in this book. We will lay out your road map to success, but it will be up to you to start moving toward your destination.

As we saw earlier, it's easier to learn something conceptually than it is to actually do it. Taking action requires courage, steadfastness and a willingness to fail, as well as the intelligence to learn from our mistakes.

We all know what it's like to try something new and fall flat on our faces in front of an important client, management or our peers. Most of the time we avoid such possibilities at all costs. But the most successful people are willing to try new things and fail many times until they get it right. It's like learning to ice skate: If you don't fall down at first, you are not trying hard enough.

It boils down to this: No amount of conceptual learning can take the place of real-world action and feedback. We can provide you with powerful strategies and tactics, but we can't provide you with the courage to act. (For some advisors, having someone along on the journey makes it a great deal easier to take action. For these advisors, enrolling in a coaching program may make a great deal of sense, as we'll discuss in Chapter 8.)

Obviously, if you don't act, you won't get the rewards that come from taking action. And if you don't take action—if this ends up being just one more business book that you read and put away on your shelf—you are unlikely to achieve the transformative changes you desire. So dig deep and find the courage to act to implement the seven strategies we will turn to next.

Ultimately, the greatest rewards come to the financial advisors who:
- Have the wisdom to seek out knowledge and guidance about what works
- Have the courage to take action despite the possibility of failure

- Are willing to accept and learn from the heat of real-world feedback
- Consistently coordinate both knowing and doing with long-term vision

If you can do these four things—and with our help we believe you can—the business of your dreams can become your everyday reality far sooner than you think.

Chapter 3
Attract Affluent Clients

Financial advisors are often taught from day one to seek out as many clients as they can and sell them as much product as possible. Unfortunately, this is rarely highly profitable. Advisors who follow this approach all too often end up with lackluster practices and unfulfilled career dreams.

We recommend a different path: working with fewer but wealthier clients. But who are these clients and what do they want from their advisors? How can you attract them so that you can build a more successful business and create a better lifestyle for yourself while effectively meeting their financial challenges?

A clear understanding of the affluent will be the foundation of your success. You will be able to identify your optimum target market niche—the affluent clients whom you can serve best and most profitably—and then to systematically position yourself to attract these clients. And by knowing exactly what the affluent want, you can implement the business model that will meet their most important financial needs.

The Affluent: A Demographic Profile

In 2005, industry researcher Russ Alan Prince headed up a survey of 1,417 individuals with between $500,000 and $5 million in liquid assets and a net worth between $1 million and $10 million.

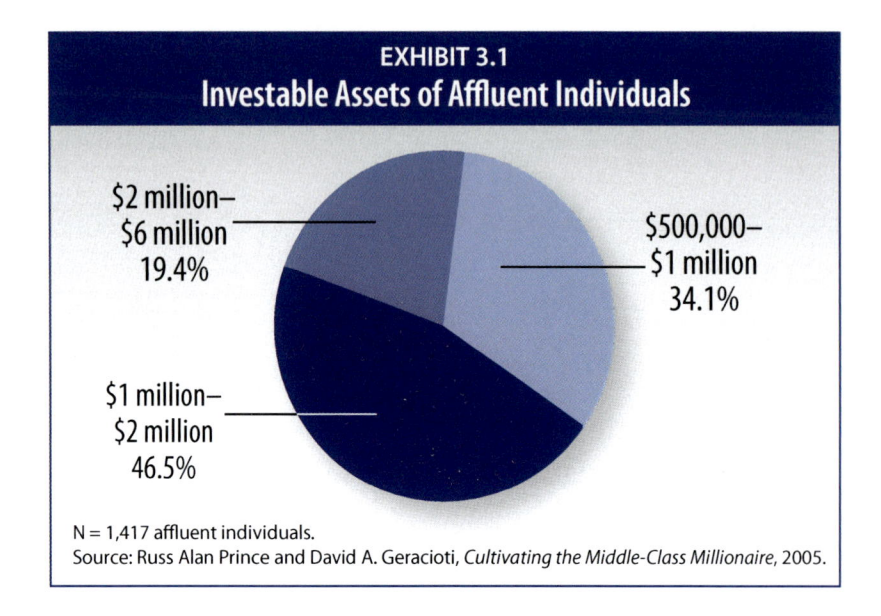

> **EXHIBIT 3.1**
> **Investable Assets of Affluent Individuals**
>
> - $500,000–$1 million: 34.1%
> - $1 million–$2 million: 46.5%
> - $2 million–$6 million: 19.4%
>
> N = 1,417 affluent individuals.
> Source: Russ Alan Prince and David A. Geracioti, *Cultivating the Middle-Class Millionaire*, 2005.

As **Exhibit 3.1** shows, nearly two-thirds of those surveyed (65.9 percent) have more than $1 million in investable assets. Take a step back, let this number sink in and stop worrying about there not being enough affluent individuals for you to work with. Start thinking bigger and better (clients), and soon your business will be bigger and better as well.

Now, to really understand and best serve affluent clients, it is total assets, not just investable assets, that you are interested in. A look at net worth, as shown in **Exhibit 3.2**, reinforces the positive picture about the level of affluence in the United States. Just over half (53.9 percent) of the survey group each have a net worth between $1 million and $3 million, while 46.1 percent each have a net worth between $3 million and $10 million.

Surprisingly, very few affluent individuals actually think of themselves as being wealthy but instead view themselves as being middle- or upper-middle-class. In fact, as **Exhibit 3.3** shows, none of those surveyed classified themselves as being wealthy, and 42.6 percent thought they were

EXHIBIT 3.2
Net Worth of Affluent Individuals

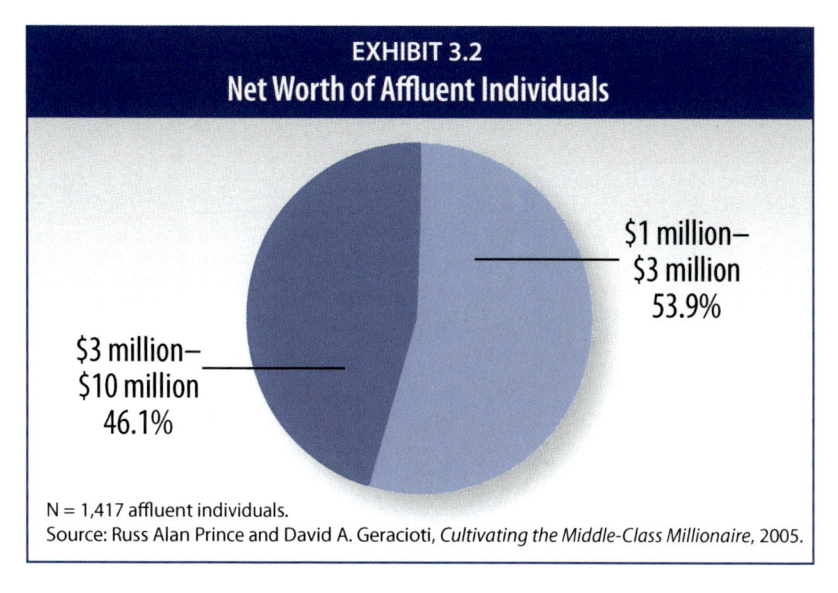

- $1 million–$3 million: 53.9%
- $3 million–$10 million: 46.1%

N = 1,417 affluent individuals.
Source: Russ Alan Prince and David A. Geracioti, *Cultivating the Middle-Class Millionaire*, 2005.

just middle-class. As you begin to attract and work with affluent clients, remember that unless they are in the ultra-high-net-worth range, with a net worth of perhaps $25 million or higher, they are likely to solidly identify with the values, concerns and dreams of the middle class.

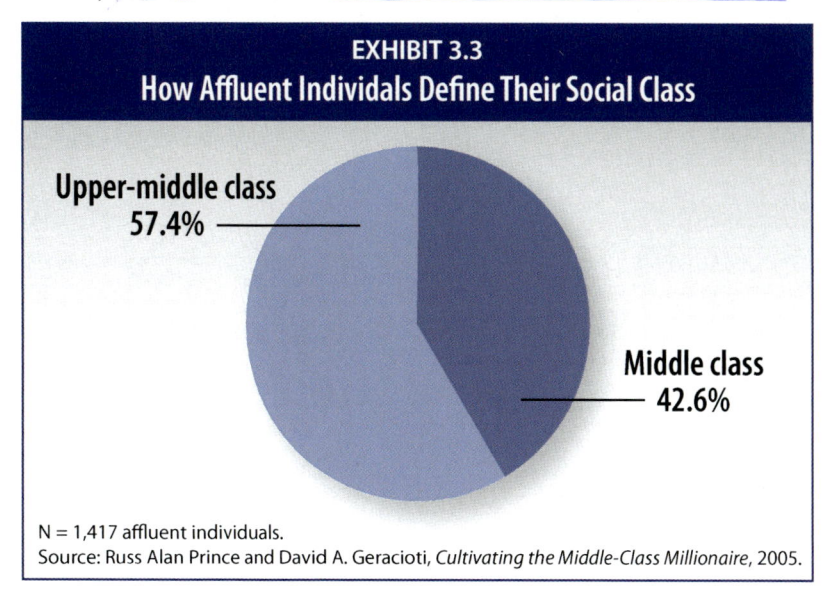

EXHIBIT 3.3
How Affluent Individuals Define Their Social Class

- Upper-middle class: 57.4%
- Middle class: 42.6%

N = 1,417 affluent individuals.
Source: Russ Alan Prince and David A. Geracioti, *Cultivating the Middle-Class Millionaire*, 2005.

EXHIBIT 3.4
Ages of Affluent Individuals

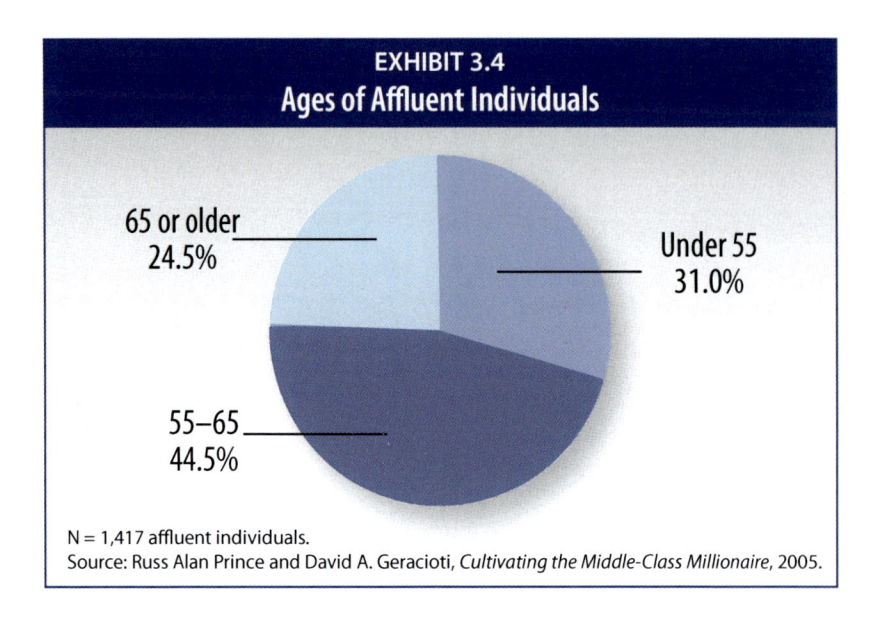

- 65 or older: 24.5%
- Under 55: 31.0%
- 55–65: 44.5%

N = 1,417 affluent individuals.
Source: Russ Alan Prince and David A. Geracioti, *Cultivating the Middle-Class Millionaire*, 2005.

EXHIBIT 3.5
Source of Wealth of Affluent Individuals

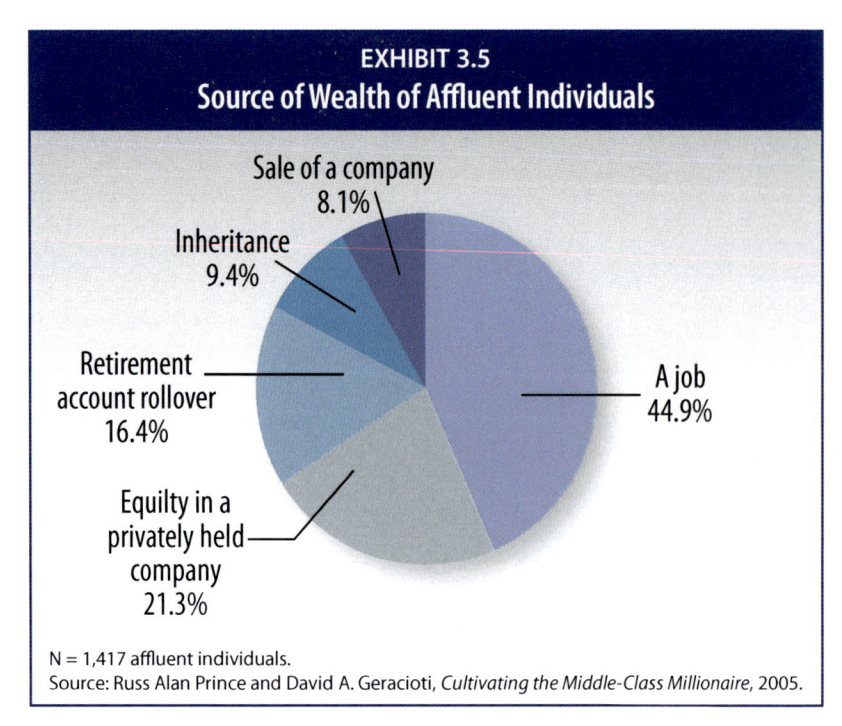

- Sale of a company: 8.1%
- Inheritance: 9.4%
- Retirement account rollover: 16.4%
- Equity in a privately held company: 21.3%
- A job: 44.9%

N = 1,417 affluent individuals.
Source: Russ Alan Prince and David A. Geracioti, *Cultivating the Middle-Class Millionaire*, 2005.

What about the ages of the affluent? It's generally difficult to accumulate wealth when one is young, so it's not surprising, as **Exhibit 3.4** shows, that only 31.0 percent of those surveyed were under 55. As for gender, 67.8 percent of those surveyed were male.

Next, although many of us assume that a great number of wealthy people have inherited their wealth, **Exhibit 3.5** shows that only 9.4 percent of those surveyed did so. Instead, the great majority made their wealth the old-fashioned way, through a job or through some kind of ongoing business endeavor.

WATCH THE VIDEO ▶ **Understanding the Affluent**
With Jonathan Powell
www.cegworldwide.com/btbook/undertanding-affluent

Nine High-Net-Worth Personalities

Many financial advisors tend to treat all affluent clients the same, but this is a mistake. If you have ever taken a personality profile test, such as the Myers-Briggs, you recognize the value of methodically classifying individuals according to different psychological types. Research from Russ Alan Prince on the psychographic characteristics of the affluent, which includes a psychological framework that parses wealthy individuals into nine high-net-worth psychological types, is useful for understanding the often subtle differences between affluent individuals. Our real-world experience confirms that while everyone has characteristics of more than one high-net-worth personality, virtually every individual has a dominant personality type along these lines.

This psychological framework applies to every aspect of attracting and serving affluent clients. It will also give you a window into many "why" questions: Why do the affluent choose the financial advisors they do, and why do they switch advisors? Why do some have many advisors and others only one? Why do the affluent prefer certain services over others?

Exhibit 3.6 shows the distribution of the high-net-worth personality types, and **Exhibit 3.7** gives a summary overview of each type. Two things are particularly worth noting. First, more than one-third of affluent individuals can be classified as Family Stewards, whose name alone immediately reveals some of what is most important to them. Second, while the three types that are most interested in investing per se—the Accumulators, Gamblers and Innovators—together constitute only 15.2 percent of the affluent, these prospective clients not only most frequently show up at public workshops and respond to direct mail, they also tend to be the most demanding and time-consuming of all clients. Caveat advisor!

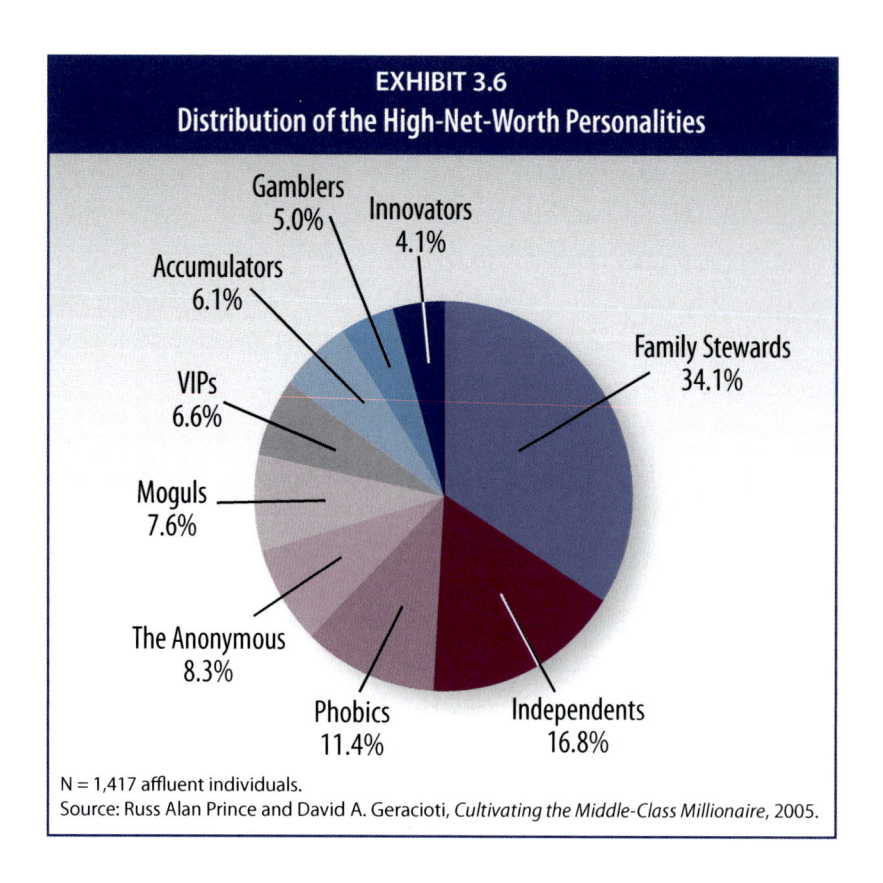

EXHIBIT 3.6
Distribution of the High-Net-Worth Personalities

- Gamblers 5.0%
- Innovators 4.1%
- Accumulators 6.1%
- VIPs 6.6%
- Moguls 7.6%
- The Anonymous 8.3%
- Phobics 11.4%
- Independents 16.8%
- Family Stewards 34.1%

N = 1,417 affluent individuals.
Source: Russ Alan Prince and David A. Geracioti, *Cultivating the Middle-Class Millionaire*, 2005.

EXHIBIT 3.7
The Nine High-Net-Worth Personalities

Family Stewards
- Dominant focus is to take care of their families.
- Conservative in personal and professional life.
- Not very knowledgeable about investing.

Independents
- Seek the personal freedom money makes possible.
- Feel investing is a necessary means to an end.
- Not interested in the process of investing or wealth management.

Phobics
- Are confused and frustrated by the responsibility of wealth.
- Dislike managing finances and avoid technical discussion of it.
- Choose advisors based on level of personal trust they feel.

The Anonymous
- Confidentiality is their prominent concern.
- Prize privacy for their financial affairs.
- Likely to concentrate assets with an advisor who protects them.

Moguls
- Control is a primary concern.
- Investing is another way of extending personal power.
- Decisive in decisions; rarely look back.

VIPs
- Investing results in ability to purchase status possessions.
- Prestige is important.
- Like to affiliate with institutions and advisors with leading reputations.

Accumulators
- Focused on making their portfolios bigger.
- Investments are performance-oriented.
- Tend to live below their means and spend frugally.

Gamblers
- Enjoy investing for the excitement of it.
- Tend to be very knowledgeable and involved.
- Exhibit a high risk tolerance.

Innovators
- Focused on leading-edge products and services.
- Sophisticated investors who like complex products.
- Tends to be technically savvy and highly educated.

Source: Russ Alan Prince and Brett Van Bortel, *The Millionaire's Advisor*™, 2003.

> **WATCH THE VIDEO** ▶ **Nine High-Net-Worth Personality Types**
> With Jonathan Powell
> www.cegworldwide.com/btbook/nine-personality-types

Key Concerns of the Affluent

The better we understand the key concerns of affluent clients and prospective clients, the better we can deliver an experience that exceeds their expectations. To begin with, although many financial advisors think their job is to create wealth, **Exhibit 3.8** clearly shows that the great majority of affluent clients are quite concerned about losing their wealth. But additional research shows that just 15.4 percent of 512 advisors surveyed believe that 20 percent or more of their affluent clients are very concerned about losing their wealth. And interestingly, individuals who identify themselves as upper-middle class feel even more strongly about this issue: The higher their perceived social class, the more concerned they are with holding on to their wealth. As an advisor to the affluent, then, your first commandment is to assist clients in preserving their wealth.

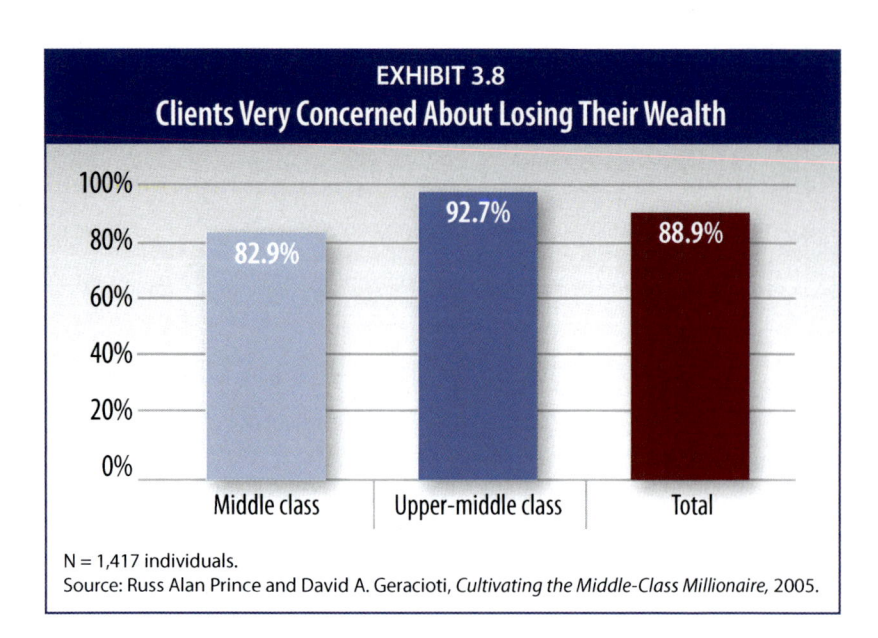

EXHIBIT 3.8
Clients Very Concerned About Losing Their Wealth

Middle class	Upper-middle class	Total
82.9%	92.7%	88.9%

N = 1,417 individuals.
Source: Russ Alan Prince and David A. Geracioti, *Cultivating the Middle-Class Millionaire*, 2005.

EXHIBIT 3.9
Clients' Concerns About Tax Mitigation

Tax Concern	Net Worth		Total
	$1 million - $3 million	$3 million - $10 million	
Mitigating income taxes	90.1%	77.3%	84.7%
Mitigating estate taxes	21.7%	81.3%	49.2%
Mitigating capital gains taxes	27.1%	58.5%	41.7%

N = 1,417 individuals. Source: Russ Alan Prince and David A. Geracioti, *Cultivating the Middle-Class Millionaire*, 2005.

Another key issue is tax mitigation. As **Exhibit 3.9** shows, mitigating income taxes is a concern of more than 90 percent of those with a net worth between $1 million and $3 million and of more than three-quarters of those with a net worth between $3 million and $10 million. For those in the higher net-worth range, mitigating estate and capital gains taxes is also a major concern.

Of course the affluent have many other concerns, as **Exhibit 3.10** shows. These range from ensuring that heirs, parents, children and grandchildren are taken care of to having adequate medical insurance, legal protection, personal security and retirement funding. Note that there are some significant (and sometimes counterintuitive) differences between the two different net-worth categories.

It's clear that the affluent have a broad range of concerns and interests. To help you begin to effectively address such a wide range of issues, we break them down into these five categories:

1. **Wealth preservation.** From the point of view of affluent individuals, wealth preservation is not about just not losing money. It's about having

enough money to fund their lifestyles—to be able to do what they want to do, whether that's simply to retire securely and pay for their children's education or to take care of multiple homes, a boat and a jet. The way they achieve this is through astute investment management that produces optimal returns consistent with the client's time frame and tolerance for risk. Thus, wealth preservation is the primary area of focus for most financial advisors.

2. **Wealth enhancement.** The goal of wealth enhancement is to minimize the tax impact on clients' investment returns while ensuring the cash flow they need.

3. **Wealth transfer.** This is about finding and facilitating the most tax-efficient way to pass assets to a spouse and succeeding generations in ways that meet the client's wishes.

EXHIBIT 3.10
Clients' Concerns About Personal Interests and Responsibilities

Interest or Responsibility	Net Worth $1 million - $3 million	Net Worth $3 million - $10 million	Total
Ensuring that heirs are taken care of	66.9%	93.6%	79.2%
Having adequate medical insurance	78.1%	76.4%	77.3%
Having enough money in retirement	87.3%	53.0%	71.5%
Paying for children's or grandchildren's education	65.2%	28.6%	48.3%
Being sued	37.4%	58.8%	47.3%
Losing job or business	48.4%	30.5%	40.0%
Having high-quality personal security	17.8%	40.4%	28.2%
Taking care of parents	38.4%	16.1%	28.1%
Making meaningful gifts to charity	21.9%	34.8%	27.8%

N = 1,417 individuals.
Source: Russ Alan Prince and David A. Geracioti, *Cultivating the Middle-Class Millionaire*, 2005.

4. **Wealth protection.** This includes all concerns about protecting the client's wealth against catastrophic loss, potential creditors, litigants, children's spouses and potential ex-spouses, and identity thieves.

5. **Charitable giving.** This encompasses all issues related to fulfilling the client's charitable goals in the most impactful way possible. It can often support efforts in other areas of concern.

In Chapter 4 we will show you the consultative process that we teach financial advisors in our coaching programs. They have found this process to be extremely effective not only in addressing the concerns of their affluent clients, but in capturing many billions of dollars in assets under management.

Importantly, additional research conducted by CEG Worldwide shows that there is a consistent disconnect between client concerns and advisors' perceptions of client concerns. This holds true whether the topic is wealth preservation, tax mitigation or the concerns listed in **Exhibit 3.10**.

Exhibit 3.11 highlights one very important disconnect between clients and advisors. Regardless of their level of investable assets, more than 70 percent of surveyed affluent individuals are concerned about working with a high-quality investment advisor, while on average just 11.9 percent of those surveyed are concerned with diversifying their investment portfolios. By contrast, another study found that 33.4 percent of 512 surveyed advisors believe that diversifying their investment portfolios is very important to their affluent clients.

So even though diversifying an investment portfolio and creating a proper asset allocation is today universally recognized as the hallmark of competent investment management, it's simply not as important to clients and potential clients as the perceived quality and expertise of their financial advisors. To grow a great business serving delighted affluent clients, the business model you design and the client experiences you deliver must start with where the client is, not with where we are or where we think the client is.

EXHIBIT 3.11
Clients' Investment Management Concerns

Concern	Investable Assets			Total
	$500,000 - $1 million	$1 million - $2 million	$2 million - $6 million	
Working with a high-quality investment advisor	70.4%	73.7%	74.2%	72.7%
Diversifying investment portfolios	18.2%	11.2%	2.5%	11.9%

N = 1,417 individuals.
Source: Russ Alan Prince and David A. Geracioti, *Cultivating the Middle-Class Millionaire*, 2005.

WATCH THE VIDEO ▶ **The Top Five Concerns of the Affluent**
With Jonathan Powell
www.cegworldwide.com/btbook/top-five-concerns

Identify Your Target Market Niche

With a clear idea of who the affluent are, it's time for you to make a critical decision: Exactly which types of affluent clients do you want to work with? Both you and your clients will be better off if you choose to work with fewer, wealthier clients. All of you will enjoy a wide variety of benefits when you pare down your clientele to a specific market niche.

Your clients will be better-served because you will have the depth of expertise required to recognize and either directly offer or otherwise find solutions for their specific needs and challenges. You will be better-off because you will need to put together just one set of adaptable solutions, services and strategic partners, freeing up your time to further focus on client relationships. And as you become known within your niche as the expert best able to meet the specific needs of your community, you are more likely to receive strong referrals. In short, when you specialize in a niche market, it's easier to become the expert your clients need and to position yourself as the expert your clients want, and it's easier and more cost-effective to provide world-class service that directly addresses all of your clients' needs.

A practice devoted to a specific client niche is almost always also a more enjoyable practice. When you work with one type of client whom you have consciously chosen, and whom you truly have an affinity for, you will likely be happier both on and off the job and much less likely to get "burned out." Your quality of life as an advisor will rise dramatically because you will be working with people you like, are interested in and have an affinity for.

We've seen this not only in the financial advisors we coach, but also in our research. A survey we conducted in 2011 of elite financial advisors (those with at least $50 million in assets under management and five years

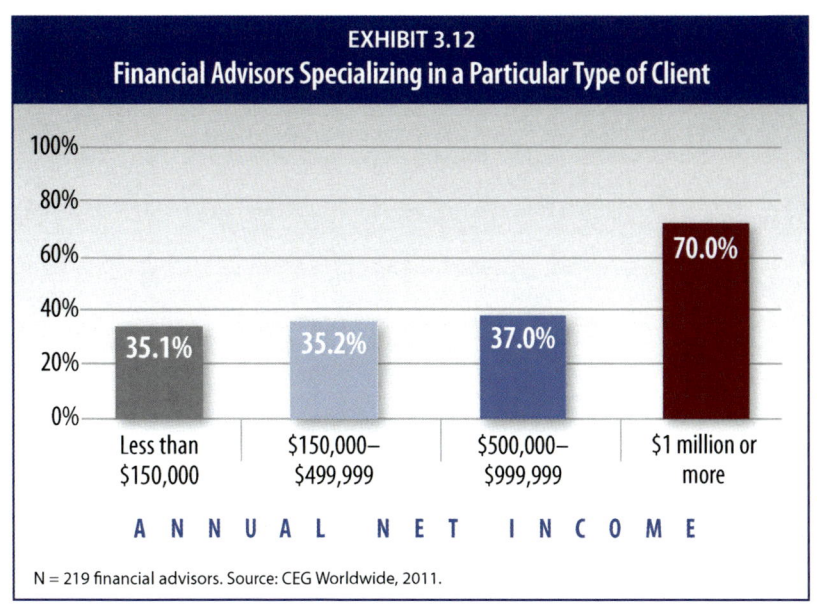

EXHIBIT 3.12
Financial Advisors Specializing in a Particular Type of Client

Annual Net Income	Percentage
Less than $150,000	35.1%
$150,000–$499,999	35.2%
$500,000–$999,999	37.0%
$1 million or more	70.0%

N = 219 financial advisors. Source: CEG Worldwide, 2011.

of experience as an advisor) found a clear correlation between advisor net income and proclivity to specialize in a particular type of client. As you can see in **Exhibit 3.12**, the financial advisors earning more than $1 million a year were twice as likely as all other advisors to specialize.

If you think of a "niche" as a defined market that is particularly well-suited to your talents, skills and interests, then, as **Exhibit 3.13** suggests, there are a mind-boggling number of potential niches. Choose a niche that you are passionate about, and don't be afraid to pioneer a brand-new niche.

EXHIBIT 3.13
Affluent Segments, with Specific Niche Examples

Affluent Segment	Examples of Specific Niches Within Segment
Self-employed professionals	Radiologists, consultants, M&A attorneys
Independent salespeople	Financial product wholesalers, Gulfstream jet aircraft salespeople, medical device salespeople
Key corporate executives	Google, Exxon or AT&T senior executives
Artists and entertainers	Behind-the-camera television talent, screenplay writers, best-selling novelists
Professional athletes	Retired San Francisco 49ers stars, Atlanta Flames hockey players
Successful business builders	Local developers of high-end homes, 20-store McDonald's franchise owners
Prudent retirees (with $1 million or more in retirement funds)	Hewlett-Packard retirees, Lockheed Martin retirees, Chevron retirees
Widows	Widows with large estates working with the top local estate planning attorneys
Divorcees	Divorcees with large settlements working with the top local divorce planning attorneys
Inheritors	High-end estate planning attorneys in local market, local support groups for sudden wealth

Source: CEG Worldwide.

WATCH THE VIDEO ▶ **Find Your Perfect Niche**
With John Bowen
www.cegworldwide.com/btbook/find-your-perfect-niche

The trick is to relentlessly drill down to find the market niche that bests suits your skills and personality. Whom, in the best possible of all worlds, would you like to work with most? To whom could you provide so much value that it becomes easy to build the wealth management business of your dreams?

Once you have answered these questions, do some research to determine whether a particular niche really makes sense for you. We recommend this four-step process:

1. Identify several concentrations or sources of wealth in your geographic area.

2. Identify a few potential niche markets where you can add value and are likely to enjoy working with clients.

3. Interview centers of influence (COIs)—movers and shakers in the niche—as well as any niche members among your existing client base to identify significant potential opportunities.

4. Analyze your opportunities, choose a single primary niche and make it so!

The first step is the easiest. There are concentrations of wealth everywhere. Open your eyes, ears and mind to what's around you. (If you live in the middle of Iowa, your inquiry may need to embrace a larger geographic area than if you live in Manhattan.) If you live in Charlotte, North Carolina, consider executives from banking and related industries. If you live in Ann Arbor, Michigan, consider college professors, startup scientists or university administrators. If you live in Fort Lauderdale, Florida, consider retirees, widows and yacht owners.

Once you have laid out some broad possibilities, identify one or more niches in which you believe you can add substantial value and would enjoy working. If you enjoy your clients, the odds that you'll be energized by your work (and even more important, that you will have fun while doing it) go up dramatically. Later we will discuss the number of contacts highly satisfied affluent clients have with their primary financial advisors and what those contacts entail. For now, understand that you will need to talk about much more than just their investments, so look for niches where affluent individuals and you are likely to have interests in common.

Next, talk to the centers of influence in the niche or niches you are considering. COIs are the people around whom members of the niche naturally congregate. Your objective will be to build a community around these individuals, so you need to choose a niche in which you will be able to reach many prospective affluent clients where they work, play or otherwise get together. Interviewing COIs will help you accurately determine the viability of the niche and whether your initial understanding of the niche matches up to reality. (The sidebar below provides detail on conducting effective COI interviews.)

If any of your existing clients are members of the niche, ask them for their perspectives on the niche generally and specifically how they feel an advisor could better serve those in that niche. Also ask for introductions to others in the niche, especially COIs.

The final step is to evaluate all the information you gathered and choose the best niche: one that offers significant opportunities yet is narrow enough for you to focus on effectively. While a few advisors "fall into" superb niches by accident, it generally takes a lot of hard work to determine the right niche and commit to making it your own.

Identifying and Interviewing Centers of Influence

The most effective way to determine a niche's size and depth, how to best market to those in the niche, and the unique needs and challenges of its members is to interview centers of influence—the niche's movers and shakers. COIs are highly visible and influential individuals who have in-depth niche knowledge and are typically either niche members themselves or otherwise professionally related to the niche. Be creative when seeking out COIs, as there are trade organizations, consultants and affinity groups for nearly every conceivable area of interest. Look for key individuals such as these:

- Trade association executives and affinity group leaders
- Trade press publishers, editors and reporters
- Lawyers, accountants, consultants and other professionals specializing in the niche
- Leaders and esteemed niche members

Once you have determined an initial list of three to five COIs, the hardest part for most advisors is picking up the phone and requesting a meeting. Simply explain to the COI that you are a financial advisor doing research on a specific niche and that his or her name has come up as someone who is both knowledgeable and influential. State that you'd like to discuss over lunch the unique needs of those in the niche, and then suggest a convenient date, time and place. Almost no one will say no to a request that is both earnest and flattering, and for the price of a meal you will get focused, in-depth market research.

Prepare for the interview by carefully constructing a set of specific but open-ended questions that build on what you already know about the niche. Cover the following areas:

- The primary challenges faced by niche members
- The size of the niche and the approximate average wealth of niche members
- The best ways to market to niche members
- Other professionals who specialize in offering services to the niche
- The trade, social, community and affinity groups and organizations that members of the niche and their spouses belong to
- Who your competitors in the niche are, along with their value propositions
- Industry events and publications of interest to niche members
- The identity of other niche COIs and other professional advisors to niche members (attorneys, accountants, etc.)

Close every COI interview with two final questions: "If you were me, knowing what you now know, what else should I have asked you?" and "May I give you a call if any additional questions come up?" Follow up after the meeting with a handwritten thank-you note. If the interview results in any specific successes, send another note or give the COI a call to keep him or her in the loop.

Narrow It Down Once More: Define Your Ideal Client Profile

Once you have defined the niche on which you will focus, create yet another filter for the clients with whom you'll work. Define an ideal client profile, a detailed description of the clients within your niche whom you want to work with. It should include the following information:

- **A general description of your ideal client.** Include stage of life (working vs. retired), industry, occupation, specific company and job (if appropriate), marital status, education level, age range, and any other relevant demographic characteristics.

- **The geographic location of your ideal clients.** Don't spread yourself too thin.

- **Amount of investable assets.** Don't shoot too low here! Advisors often don't realize how easily they can move upmarket if they are willing to set the bar high. One useful guideline is the "Rule of Five." Take the top 20 percent of your clients, calculate their average investable assets and then multiply that figure by five.

- **Minimum assets under management and minimum fee.** Our research consistently shows that financial advisors who set higher investment minimums and have minimum fees have higher incomes.

- **Financial challenges.** What financial challenges are you most interested in helping solve? Be specific here.

- **Source of acquisition.** How do you want your ideal client to come to you? Referrals? Strategic alliances? Seminars? Credibility marketing?

- **High-net-worth personality, compatibility and profitability.** Which of the high-net-worth personality types are you likely to work best with? Whom should you avoid?

- **Personal enjoyment and affinity.** What kind of affluent clients will you most enjoy working with? With whom do you share the most interests and avocations?

Summarize your ideal client profile on a single page. And while you're at it, think about things from the opposite direction: For what kind of affluent client in your chosen niche would you, with all your personality strengths and flaws, be just the right kind of advisor? The answer should be exactly the same.

Position Yourself as an Expert

In Chapter 5 we will show you how to effectively grow your assets and attract new affluent clients who fit your ideal client profile. In the meantime, it's worth considering ways of moving your marketing efforts forward once you have chosen your target market niche.

Begin by fully immersing yourself in your niche. Declare yourself as someone who is an expert in the needs of the members of your niche. Your goal is to be first in the minds of members of this community, and that means positioning yourself as the expert who delivers compelling value that niche members won't find anywhere else. There are five steps to such successful positioning:

1. Identify your *compelling value proposition*—the single most important value that you offer to your clients and that sets you apart from your competition.

2. Write your *positioning statement*—a succinct description of your compelling value proposition.

3. Create an *elevator speech*—a brief, persuasive speech that motivates prospective clients to explore doing business with you.

4. Construct a *call to action*—a specific first step you would like prospective clients to take.

5. Share your *personal story*—the reason behind why you care so much about serving your clients extremely well.

A compelling value proposition goes deeper than your specific skill set. Instead, it is the specific set of financial challenges you are particularly adept at solving. Obviously, it should be in close alignment with the needs of members of your niche. As **Exhibit 3.14** shows, the single most important criterion for the affluent in choosing an advisor is the advisor's overall expertise. Once you determine your real expertise in solving the

EXHIBIT 3.14
Selection Criteria of Affluent Individuals in Choosing Financial Advisors

Criterion	Clients Rating Criterion as Very Important
Overall expertise of advisor	91.0%
Care advisor takes to identify needs	89.0%
Investment management style	84.1%
Trust in advisor	82.0%
Discretion of advisor	81.1%
Attentiveness of advisor	80.2%
Advisor's desire to establish long-term relationship	74.2%
Reputation of advisor	65.2%
Quality of proposals	55.1%
Quality of presentations	51.9%
Quality of promotional materials	33.9%
Investment performance/track record	26.6%

Source: Russ Alan Prince and Karen Maru File, *Cultivating the Affluent*.
Analysis: CEG Worldwide.

financial challenges of your clients, you can claim this as the centerpiece of your value proposition and commit to being seen as the expert your clients want.

Next, create a succinct statement of your compelling value proposition. This should be a clear, brief description of the value that you uniquely provide to your select group of clients and prospective clients and that is designed to meet their precise needs. It's a proclamation that resonates with the members of your niche and acts as a beacon to draw them to you. Two examples are "I help clients in my niche make smart decisions about their money so they can spend more time doing what they love" and "I make work optional for my niche."

Your positioning statement must do each of the following:

1. Provide a strong promise of benefits for your ideal clients
2. Offer to solve a challenge that already exists for these clients
3. Make your offer appear different from and better than your competition's

Above all, your positioning statement must be believable. As a sanity check, make sure your statement reflects what you really do and can do and is something you feel confident and passionate about.

The third step is to craft a compelling "elevator speech"—a statement that effectively communicates your compelling value proposition in the time it takes an elevator to reach its destination, perhaps 15 seconds at most. You can also think of this as the micro-speech you'd give a prospective client at a cocktail party. Make it short, make it passionate, and practice it in front of both other people and a video camera. Once you've said it a hundred times or so it will become second nature and you will be able to flawlessly deliver it when it counts.

Fourth, construct a call to action. When prospective clients hear your elevator speech and express interest, you must be able to offer them an easy first step toward working with you. In almost every case your call to action will be to have the prospect schedule an initial meeting to explore the possibility of working with you. (We'll say much more about this first meeting in the next chapter.) Here's an example of what you might say:

> "I'd be happy to meet with you for what we call our Discovery Meeting. The purpose of this meeting would be to explore whether we are the right firm to offer you extraordinary value. We work only with a select group of clients for whom we can have a tremendous impact. If we are not the right firm for you, we'd be more than happy to refer you to one that is. Would you like to schedule a Discovery Meeting?"

Finally, once the prospect has agreed to schedule a Discovery Meeting, take a few moments to move this initial contact to a more personal level. This sets the stage for the long-term relationship you will begin to build during the Discovery Meeting.

We have found that the best way to do this is to share a brief personal story about yourself—in particular, the events behind your motivation to serve others by becoming a financial advisor. When others hear your story, it gives them insight into who you are, what you stand for and what you had to overcome to get to where you are now. Very often, this creates in them a willingness, even an eagerness, to associate with you.

Many people believe that they don't have a story worth telling or that would interest others. Be assured that every one of us has a story that will move others. And bear in mind that you can use your story not just to

WATCH THE VIDEO ▶ **Connecting Emotionally with Prospective Clients**
With John Bowen
www.cegworldwide.com/btbook/connect-emotionally-with-prospects

cement your expert positioning, but also to make a personal connection with prospective clients, clients, team members, strategic partners and anyone else who is important to your success. The world is full of experts; people are looking for a genuine emotional connection.

Pull Clients to You with Credibility Marketing

As you create and refine your positioning statement, elevator speech, call to action and personal story, begin to reinforce your status as an expert through a credibility or "pull marketing" program. Ideally, you want to pull clients toward you rather than having to chase after them. In part, this will naturally begin to happen as you build your reputation within your niche and you generate referrals from highly satisfied clients. Simultaneously, however, you want to get your name out there as the financial advisor most qualified to solve the challenges of members of your niche. We recommend these actions:

- **Review your existing marketing materials.** Assess your marketing collateral to see whether it supports your new niche-focused strategy and is in sync with your existing and potential niche clients. Review everything that reflects your brand—logo, letterhead, business cards, brochure, Web site, even the signage on your building—and jettison anything that no longer fits.

- **Write and publish a positioning package.** Create a comprehensive positioning package that describes in detail your firm's mission, history, personnel, fees, strategic alliances, wealth management philosophy and consultative process (described in the next chapter). Your positioning package should be professionally designed and visually appealing and should make clear all the benefits of working with you.

- **Build an effective Web site.** Construct a comprehensive, professional Web site that clearly communicates the special value you offer your niche. Don't skimp here and hire your nephew or simply accept the mass-manufactured Web site that your firm may offer for free. Make sure your site offers an email newsletter, and then send one out to existing and potential clients on a regular basis.

- **Write articles for your niche's trade publications.** Seek out publications that are relevant to your niche, and do your best to get published in them. In addition to asking your niche's COIs what magazines and publications they read, consult titles such as *Writer's Market*, the *Encyclopedia of Associations* and the *Gale Directory of Publications and Broadcast Media*. Your goal should be to publish at least three articles a year of from 750 to 1,500 words. Another possibility is to secure a monthly or bimonthly column in a relevant publication. Have reprints of your published articles or columns readily available for your clients and make them available on your Web site. For pull marketing purposes, trade publications within your niche are far superior to being quoted or published in the local newspaper.

- **Write and publish white papers.** Take what you have learned from your COI interviews and create white papers that address the challenges faced by those in your niche. Ideally, you should combine industry research with your own commentary and recommendations. If you're not a good writer, hire someone to help you. Once finished, distribute your white paper as widely as possible, making it available on your Web site, sending it to publications, and having professional reprints available for clients and potential clients.

- **Write and publish books.** Having a book or two with your name on it can tremendously increase your credibility, but don't take this on until you have a dozen or so articles or a few white papers under your belt. Writing and having a book published is a major undertaking, one that can all too easily distract you from your core efforts and competencies. Consider working with a professional writer on this.

- **Leverage social media.** LinkedIn is the social media network of choice for professionals and you should undoubtedly establish a presence there. To leverage it effectively, send contact requests to all of your niche's COIs, all of your clients in your niche and all members of the media working in your niche. Broaden your contacts within your niche further by inviting their contacts within your niche to join. (Do not use LinkedIn's standard contact request form, but instead send a personalized request to join someone's network—you will get a much higher rate of success and may start having a conversation right away.) Once your network is well-established, use LinkedIn to promote upcoming events such as webinars and presentations. You can also use it to promote your white papers, articles and videos, always inviting comment when you do.

- **Deliver group presentations.** Standing in front of a group of your ideal prospective clients is a very effective way to build your credibility and invite additional interaction. Develop a 30-to-60-minute presentation on a subject that your ideal clients will find compelling and that motivates them to answer a call to action to enter your consultative process. As you know, myriad seminars are offered today by financial advisors. The great majority, however, have very little to offer the affluent. Differentiate yourself by preparing and marketing your **presentations to your specific audience.**

- **Conduct webinars.** Webinars are an extremely cost-effective way to reach prospective clients. Allow for full interaction between presenter and audience through a range of tools including phone, text chat and polling. To limit the time you put toward producing new content, you can easily repurpose your live group presentation content for use in webinars.

- **Develop your own videos.** Videos are a powerful tool for connecting with members of your niche and inspiring them to take action. One of the first videos you should consider is one in which you tell your personal story. This will position you as an expert, create an emotional connection with your audience and provide a strong call to action. For examples, click here to view the personal story videos of each of the authors.

In addition to these steps, consider contacting media resources to see how feasible it is for you to appear on radio or television. Even if you can't arrange an appearance on a show relevant to your niche, the very fact that you have made appearances on radio or television will reinforce your position as an expert among both your existing and prospective clients.

In all your marketing efforts, you will need to decide whether to do the work yourself; have an employee or assistant do it; or outsource it to a

> **WATCH THE VIDEO** ▶ **Nurturing Affluent Private Clients**
> With John Bowen
> www.cegworldwide.com/btbook/nurturing-affluent-private-clients

freelance writer, marketing specialist or advertising agency. There are many online freelance marketplaces now available that can be a good alternative if you are willing to work with an individual on a virtual basis. Guru.com, Elance.com, oDesk.com and freelancer.com are perhaps the best-known. And of course, work with your compliance professional in all of your marketing efforts.

With your understanding in place of which affluent clients to work with and how to attract them to you, it's time to look at how to work with them effectively. We turn to that next.

Chapter 4
Strengthen Client Relationships

In Chapter 3 we covered *whom* you want to attract: affluent clients fitting your ideal client profile. We also discussed the importance of establishing yourself as an expert in order to begin to "pull in" prospective ideal clients.

Now we will show you *how* to work with these ideal clients and prospective clients. By using the wealth management consulting process we set out, you'll win new business and "WOW" your clients with an unprecedented level of professional focus and attention.

This chapter will show you how to build such strong client relationships that your clients aren't just satisfied, but are completely loyal to you and absolutely passionate about being your clients. Needless to say, loyal and passionate clients will give you more of their assets to manage, provide referrals for other ideal clients and generally be a pleasure to work with.

We will begin by explaining why wealth management is far and away the best business model. We'll also briefly consider what to do about your existing clients who do not fit your ideal client profile. We will then map out the consultative process in detail, including how to create a Total Client Profile by using a tool known as "mind mapping." Finally, we'll cover the mechanics of building a professional network to help deliver the range of advanced planning services that your affluent clients need and expect.

The Wealth Management Business Model

Virtually all financial advisors employ one of two business models:

1. **Investment generalists.** These financial advisors offer a broad range of investment products and do not specialize in a single type of product. While they conduct brief fact-finding sessions and then offer clients a suite of possible products based on their needs, consulting is not an essential part of their business model. Instead, they are transaction-focused.

2. **Wealth managers.** These advisors take a comprehensive approach to meeting client needs by using a highly consultative approach to construct integrated, personalized solutions.

As you know, many advisors these days call themselves "wealth managers." One of our studies showed that 46.3 percent of surveyed financial advisors identified themselves as wealth managers, while the remainder (53.7 percent) identified themselves according to their investment orientation, such as financial advisor, investment advisor, investment expert or financial planner. However, the study showed that only 6.6 percent of the advisors actually are wealth managers. The remainder, or 93.4 percent, are investment-oriented. (**See Exhibit 4.1.**)

Why do so many advisors want to be *seen* as wealth managers even though they really aren't? Perhaps it's because true wealth managers are, on average, far more successful than investment generalists.

As **Exhibit 4.2** shows, while wealth managers on average have far fewer clients than investment generalists do, their average assets under management or administration are more than twice as great. Even more revealing is the fact that wealth managers, on average, earn more than three times as much as investment generalists ($881,000 vs. $279,000 per year). These, of course, are only averages, and many wealth managers actually do far better than this.

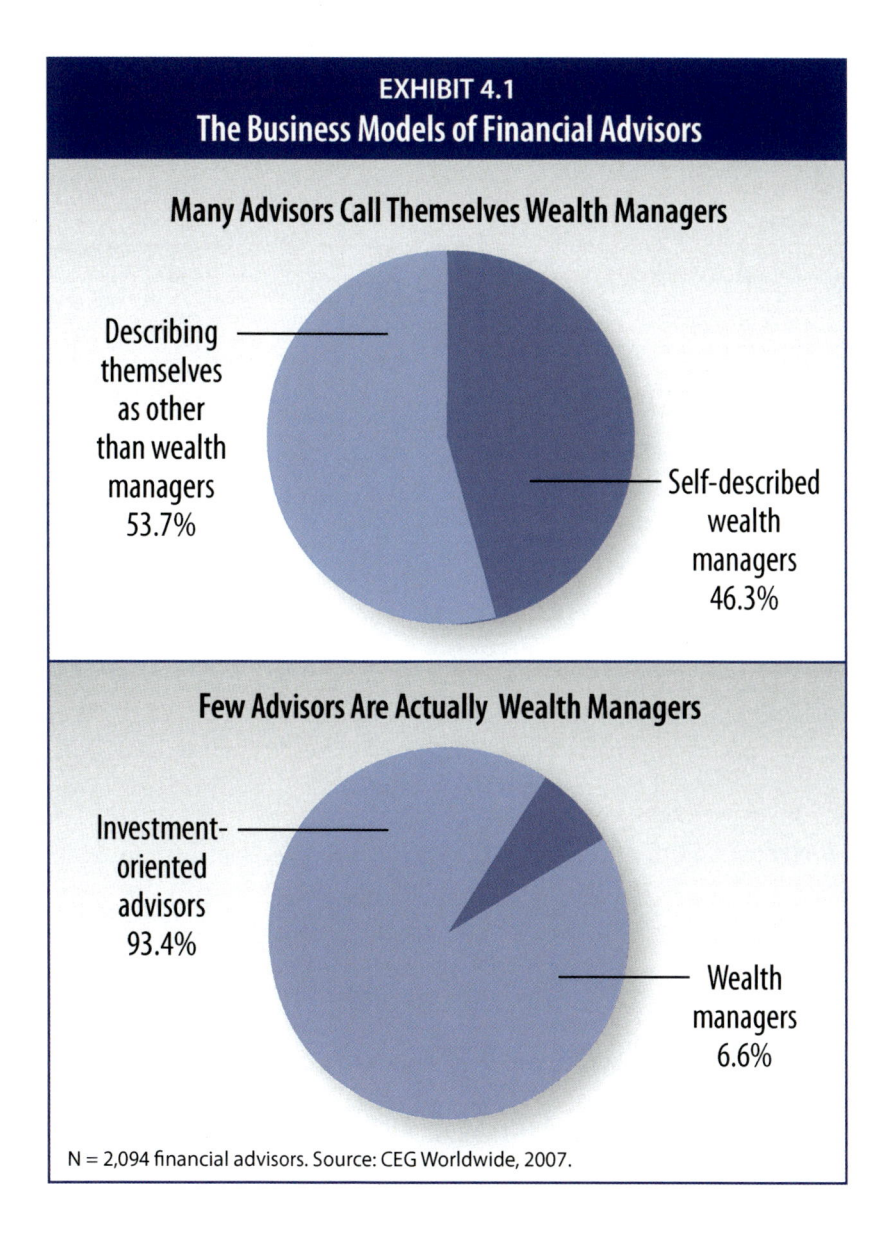

EXHIBIT 4.1
The Business Models of Financial Advisors

Many Advisors Call Themselves Wealth Managers

- Describing themselves as other than wealth managers 53.7%
- Self-described wealth managers 46.3%

Few Advisors Are Actually Wealth Managers

- Investment-oriented advisors 93.4%
- Wealth managers 6.6%

N = 2,094 financial advisors. Source: CEG Worldwide, 2007.

EXHIBIT 4.2
The Two Business Models Compared

	Business Model	
	Investment Generalist	Wealth Manager
Average assets under administration	$307.8 million	$645.2 million
Average annual net income	$279,000	$881,000
Average number of clients	269.3	101.1

N = 2,094 financial advisors. Source: CEG Worldwide, 2007.

WATCH THE VIDEO ▶ **Profile in Success: Mary Brooks**
Walnut Creek, California
www.cegworldwide.com/btbook/mary-brooks

A Deeper Look at Wealth Management

In Chapter 3 we discussed the kind of services and the client experience that affluent individuals are looking for. Assuming that the affluent vote with their feet and their pocketbooks, it's clear from **Exhibit 4.2** that wealth management is indeed the business model that affluent clients strongly prefer. Let's take an in-depth look, then, at what wealth management really means.

At its core, wealth management (WM) comprises investment consulting (IC) plus advanced planning (AP) plus relationship management (RM). In shorthand:

$$WM = IC + AP + RM$$

As our formula shows, investment consulting is the first element of wealth management. As you will recall from Chapter 3, wealth preservation—which is achieved through astute investment management—is the first of the five key financial concerns of the affluent.

Whether financial advisors manage investments on their own, turn to other professionals or work with a TAMP (turnkey asset management provider), 100 percent of them provide investment consulting (although some do it better than others). This means that differentiating yourself from your competition through investment management alone is very difficult, if not impossible.

The second component is advanced planning, which addresses the other four major financial concerns of the affluent: wealth enhancement (WE), wealth transfer (WT), wealth protection (WP) and charitable giving (CG), as expressed by this formula:

AP = WE + WT + WP + CG

None of the five areas of concern stands in isolation from the rest. Wealth protection, for example, is often intertwined with wealth transfer needs. And charitable giving can often support goals in each of the other four areas. To be most effective in assisting your clients, you need to help them deal with each area systematically while maintaining an integrated approach to their overall financial pictures.

Most advisors who claim to be wealth managers often provide only investment consulting. They provide any additional services on a reactive basis. Offering advanced planning services therefore represents a major opportunity to differentiate yourself. But don't overpromise. For example, you must already have an extended expert network (as we describe later in this chapter) in place or well under way before you can effectively provide the range of advanced planning services.

The final component that ties wealth management together is relationship management (RM). This, in turn, consists of CRM (client relationship management) and ERM (expert relationship management). This is our shorthand:

RM = CRM + ERM

Client relationship management in the wealth management model means forging in-depth, collaborative and consultative client relationships. But since affluent clients these days recognize that no one can be an expert in everything, they want their primary advisors to work closely with the experts whom they already have onboard (such as their accountants and lawyers) as well as additional experts whom their advisors will bring to the party from their own networks.

Relationship management involves three key tasks:

1. Building deep client relationships that will allow you to fully understand your clients' most important financial challenges and dreams. This, in turn, will enable you to effectively meet all their needs. The best means for building these types of relationship is the consultative process.

2. Assembling and managing a network of your own experts (including lawyers, insurance experts and so on) so that you can bring to bear the exact expertise that your clients need.

3. Working with the professional advisors your affluent clients already have, such as attorneys and accountants, as well as other financial advisors managing other parts of their finances.

WATCH THE VIDEO ▶ **The Wealth Management Formula**
With John Bowen
www.cegworldwide.com/btbook/wealth-management-formula

As a wealth manager, you will become what your affluent clients really want you to be: their personal chief financial officer, someone who helps them think through their challenges while working with them collaboratively to determine and implement optimal solutions. We turn next to using the consultative process to build exactly this type of relationship.

Releasing Inappropriate Clients

To succeed as a wealth manager, you need to work with fewer but wealthier clients. This means that you will have to let go of those clients who are not part of your target market niche or who otherwise do not fit your ideal client profile.

EXHIBIT 4.3
Four Methods for Releasing Clients

Method	Pros	Cons	The Upshot
"Quiet file" the clients	Quick, easy, immediate and inexpensive; needs no client buy-in	Problem clients rarely "fade away"; long-term compliance and legal risks; inconsistent with positioning yourself as expert	Most advisors default to this, but this is *not* the recommended course of action
Hire a junior advisor within your office to service the clients	Relatively easy to get client buy-in; advisor retains revenue stream and ultimate relationship	Must train, supervise and pay salary of new advisor; does not fundamentally address inappropriate nature of clients	Not a silver bullet, since doesn't address client's fundamental inappropriateness
Transfer the clients to an advisor in your office	Favor by branch managers; advisor may retain a portion of ongoing revenue stream	Again, does not address clients' inappropriate nature; clients may demand orginal advisor's attention	Branch managers often eager to help facilitate this
Sell the business of the unsuitable clients to an advisor in another firm	Truly addresses inappropriate clients; advisor receives immediate and perhaps earn-out revenue	Takes time and focus to value clients, negotiate a deal and assist in transfer process	Best possible option; consulting firms available to facilitate

Source: CEG Worldwide.

Once you have determined whom you should let go, you may still find yourself reluctant to actually release certain clients, especially if they have been with you for a long time. But the truth is, if they aren't the right clients for you, then you are almost certainly not the right financial advisor for them, and keeping them on as clients is actually doing them a disservice. These clients will receive more value by working with someone else, perhaps someone who is newer in the business or who specializes in clients just like them. When such clients are turned over to a more appropriate advisor, the typical response is "Thank you for referring me elsewhere." They are quite happy to get the services and value they need from the right advisor.

What's the best way to release clients? As **Exhibit 4.3** shows, you have four choices. The most common method—"quiet filing" clients—is the worst possible choice because it rarely works and ultimately amounts to just ignoring the problem. The best possible method is to sell the business of the unsuitable clients to another financial advisor.

Such sales are increasingly common, and a number of consulting firms specialize in facilitating these kinds of transactions. An earn-out will often be part of the deal. You might receive a certain percentage of the previous year's revenue associated with the sold clients, plus an amount equal to that over the next one to two years. The downside here is that it takes time and energy to value your clients and then find an outside advisor whom you feel good about and who is willing to pay a fair price. The upside is that this method truly takes inappropriate clients off your plate and can put them in the hands of an advisor better able to service them.

By releasing less-than-ideal and otherwise inappropriate clients, you will free up a tremendous amount of productive time to focus on attracting new clients and servicing existing clients. You will also dramatically improve your self-image. It's critical, however, that you release these clients in a careful, respectful way. Put yourself in the shoes of those whom you will be releasing. Ask yourself what kind of treatment you would want in this situation, from timely notice to a sensible explanation of why it is better for everyone involved to a handwritten thank-you note for the business that you provided over the years.

WATCH THE VIDEO ▶ **Learn to Let Go**
With John Bowen
www.cegworldwide.com/btbook/learn-to-let-go

The Wealth Management Consulting Process

The wealth management consulting process is a potent, field-tested way to strengthen client relationships and ensure that your affluent clients' needs are fully met. As a wealth manager, you will leverage two primary tools:

1. The Consultative Client Management (CCM) Process, consisting of a series of five different client meetings. Each is designed to foster trust, grow your relationships, and delight your prospective and existing clients. At the same time, they will provide you with numerous opportunities to gain additional assets, provide additional services and receive referrals for more clients who fit your ideal client profile. The meetings of the CCM Process are shown on the left side of **Exhibit 4.4**. As part of the CCM Process, you will use mind mapping to create a Total Client Profile, a comprehensive description of seven key areas of your client's life. Using the Total Client Profile, you will create an investment plan, and later on you will create a broader wealth management plan.

2. The expert network that will provide you with the top-end expertise that your clients need. The network and its activities are shown at the right side of **Exhibit 4.4**.

EXHIBIT 4.4
The Wealth Management Consulting Process

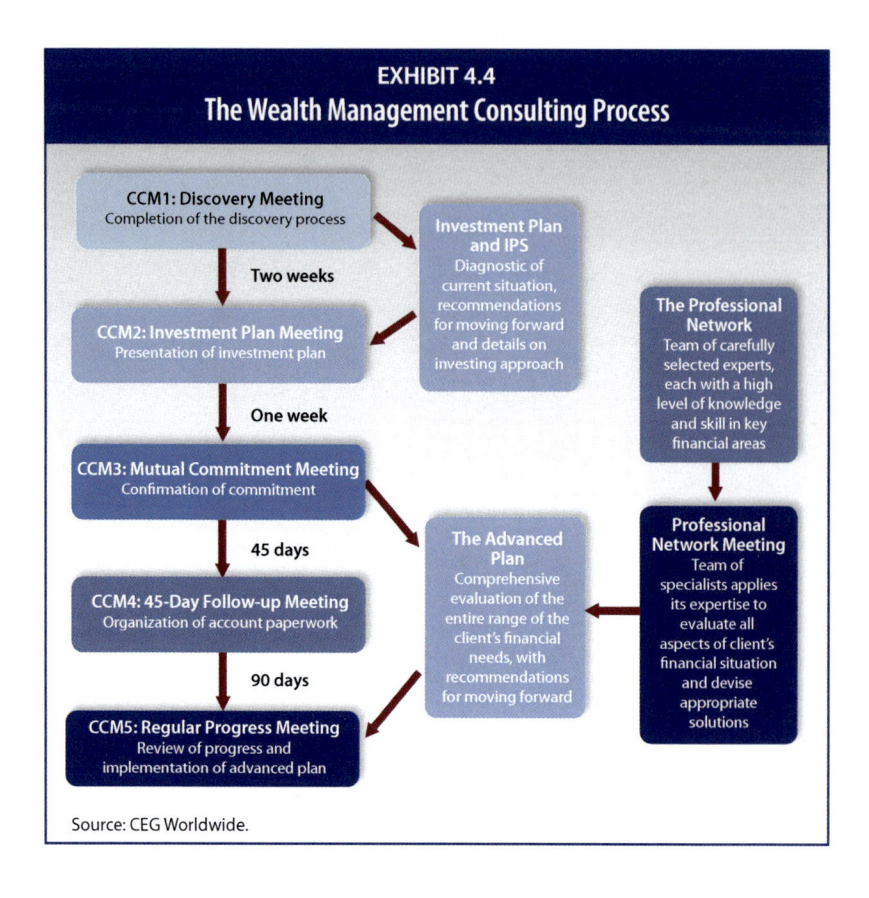

- **CCM1: Discovery Meeting** — Completion of the discovery process
  - *Two weeks* ↓
- **CCM2: Investment Plan Meeting** — Presentation of investment plan
  - *One week* ↓
- **CCM3: Mutual Commitment Meeting** — Confirmation of commitment
  - *45 days* ↓
- **CCM4: 45-Day Follow-up Meeting** — Organization of account paperwork
  - *90 days* ↓
- **CCM5: Regular Progress Meeting** — Review of progress and implementation of advanced plan

Investment Plan and IPS — Diagnostic of current situation, recommendations for moving forward and details on investing approach

The Advanced Plan — Comprehensive evaluation of the entire range of the client's financial needs, with recommendations for moving forward

The Professional Network — Team of carefully selected experts, each with a high level of knowledge and skill in key financial areas

Professional Network Meeting — Team of specialists applies its expertise to evaluate all aspects of client's financial situation and devise appropriate solutions

Source: CEG Worldwide.

We will look at the CCM Process first. Every step of this process is replicable, enabling you to consistently provide every prospective and existing client with the same high-quality experience. Knowing that they are part of a refined and well-thought-out process will bolster their confidence in you, making it more likely that they'll refer their qualified friends (who they know will also receive a top-notch experience) as well as give you additional business and remain loyal over time.

We will now take you through that client experience, beginning with your first contact with the prospect, the Discovery Meeting.

> **WATCH THE VIDEO** ▶ **The Elite Advisor Client Engagement Model**
> With John Bowen
> www.cegworldwide.com/btbook/-advisor-client-engagement-model

CCM1: Discovery Meeting

As its name suggests, this is your opportunity to discover everything that is financially important to your client. These are your objectives for the Discovery Meeting:

- To immediately establish trust by positioning yourself as an expert in addressing the financial concerns of members of your niche community

- To differentiate yourself from your competition through your superior client experience

- To uncover the prospect's most important financial issues and to determine his or her high-net-worth personality

- To collect all information necessary to assess client suitability for your services

- If appropriate, to collect all information necessary to craft an investment plan and a wealth management plan

- To begin to position yourself as the client's personal chief financial officer

- To begin to build a deeper personal connection by sharing your personal story

To ensure that the Discovery Meeting is as productive as possible, send a letter ahead of time confirming the date and time of the meeting and listing the information you'd like the prospect to bring to the meeting, such as account statements and recent income tax returns. In addition, you should also prepare an agenda for the meeting.

> **Overview of Discovery Meeting Steps**
>
> 1. Greet the prospect by name.
> 2. Acknowledge the prospect's desire to explore working together.
> 3. Explain how you will conduct the meeting.
> 4. Conduct the Total Client Profile interview, creating a mind map as you conduct the interview.
> 5. Assess whether you can add substantial value to the prospect's situation.
> 6. Describe the next steps in the process.
> 7. Define wealth management.
> 8. Tell your personal story.
> 9. Schedule the next meeting.
> 10. Send confirmation for the next meeting.

The experience starts the moment the prospect walks into your office. Remember, everything the prospect sees, hears or otherwise notices reflects directly on you. To begin, your receptionist or assistant should greet the prospect formally, by name, and offer a beverage. This shows respect and signals that you are well-prepared.

Offer appropriate beverages and reading material in your lobby. Ideally, the reading material will be copies of articles you have written, along with lifestyle magazines focused on topics of interest to your target market, such as sailing, fine architecture or luxury travel. Avoid personal finance magazines. Likewise, if you have a TV in your waiting area, play lifestyle DVDs or tune it to the Discovery Channel—not CNBC. This sets the stage for what you are all about as a financial advisor: helping your clients achieve their financial dreams.

When you greet the prospect (or existing client), remember that you are not trying to sell anything but, rather, that you are qualifying the individual as a potential client. Speaking in a respectful but not obsequious manner, say something like this:

> *"I am very much looking forward to exploring your financial goals with you to determine whether we are the right firm to help you in achieving those goals. We limit our practice to successful families in (insert your target market here) for whom we can make a significant impact. If we're not the right firm for doing this, we promise to point you in the right direction."*

Then explain how you will conduct the meeting and briefly review the agenda. By the time you have completed the Total Client Profile (which we describe below), you should be able to assess whether you can add substantial value to the prospect's situation. If you feel that you can, describe the next steps in your process and set the stage for your future relationship by defining wealth management for the client. We have found it to be very effective to do so using the formula that we provided earlier in this chapter. Then take a moment to share your personal story, focusing on why you care so much about serving your clients extremely well. Then schedule the next meeting in your process, the Investment Meeting. Finally, send a follow-up letter that reconfirms the date and time for that meeting.

> **Critical Success Factors for the Discovery Meeting**
>
> - **Be confident.** Approach the Discovery Meeting from the perspective of whether this prospect is really appropriate for your firm, in terms of both overall match to your ideal client profile and profitability potential.
>
> - **Be focused.** The meeting should be extremely focused and not last more than 90 minutes.
>
> - **Be efficient.** Recognize that the affluent already have more than enough friends. What they often really have is a shortage of time. They want professionals who are extremely efficient and effective.
>
> - **Be well-practiced.** Creating a Total Client Profile using a mind map takes a bit of practice. Ask your co-workers, family members and friends if you can practice on them first.

WATCH THE VIDEO ▶ **The Discovery Meeting**
With Paul Brunswick
www.cegworldwide.com/btbook/discovery-meeting

Creating the Total Client Profile

At the heart of the Discovery Meeting is the creation of the Total Client Profile. (See **Exhibit 4.5** for an overview of this process.) Your goal is to discover everything you possibly can about your prospective client in seven key areas:

1. **Values.** What's truly important to your prospect about money and finances? Here, and throughout the process, have questions prepared that enable you to quickly go deeper to find out how the prospect truly feels. For example, a typical answer to "What's most important to

you about your finances?" is "Financial security." Because this doesn't actually reveal very much, you can then follow up with a "second order" question like "What specifically about financial security is of most concern to you?" The prospect might respond, "Taking care of my family's health and well-being" or "Maintaining my lifestyle through retirement." These specific responses will enable you to do a better job for your prospective client.

2. **Goals.** What does the prospect want to achieve over the long run? When does he or she want to retire? How about college for any children? What about travel or a second career? What other dreams does the prospect have?

3. **Relationships.** Who really counts for your prospect? Whom does the prospect love? Who is important to your prospect, including non-family members and even pets?

4. **Assets.** In order to address the prospect's entire financial picture, you must find out what the prospect's assets are, and where and how they are held. This includes real estate, home businesses, brokerage accounts, retirement plans and so on. (Ask the prospect in advance of the meeting to bring tax returns and account records and have an assistant photocopy the records during your meeting.) Note that you ask about assets fourth, not first. This reflects your understanding that there are things more important to the prospect than money.

5. **Advisors.** Whom does the prospect rely on for advice, from CPAs and attorneys to insurance agents and other financial advisors? Find out what has worked—and what has not—in your prospect's relationships with these other advisors.

6. **Process.** How does the prospect prefer to work with his or her advisors? Once the prospect has expressed a preference, be prepared to honor

that choice for the rest of your relationship. If the prospect wants to be contacted only by email and never by phone, then that's what you must do.

7. Interests. What are the prospect's hobbies, sports and leisure activities, charitable and philanthropic involvements, religious and spiritual proclivities, and children's schools and activities? If you share an interest with your prospective client, over time you can leverage this interest to build further intimacy.

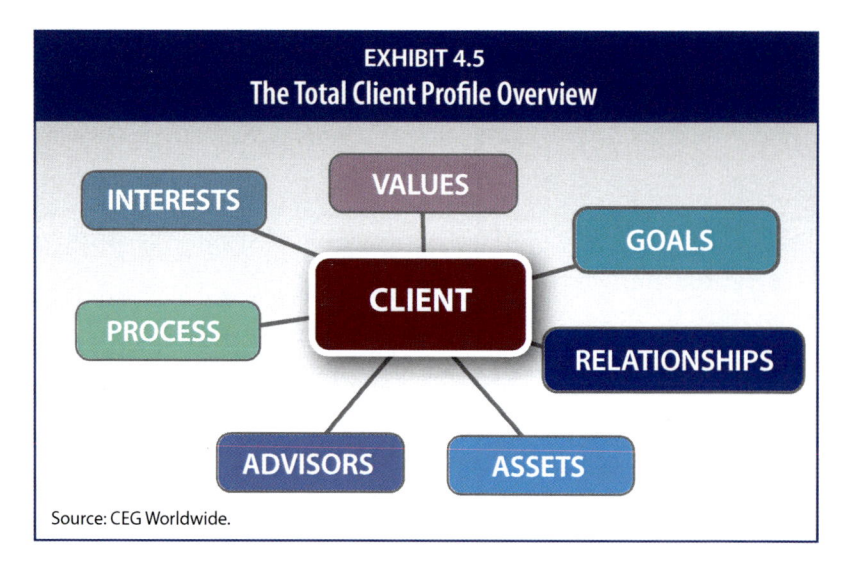

EXHIBIT 4.5
The Total Client Profile Overview

INTERESTS — VALUES — GOALS — CLIENT — PROCESS — RELATIONSHIPS — ADVISORS — ASSETS

Source: CEG Worldwide.

As you can see, your inquiry into who the prospect really is goes much further than the fact-finding process used by most advisors, which is typically limited to assets, net worth, time horizon, investment goals and risk tolerance. While these subjects are clearly important and need to be covered, they do little to reveal what really matters most to the individual (or couple) in front of you.

WATCH THE VIDEO ▶ **The Total Client Profile**
With John Bowen
www.cegworldwide.com/btbook/total-client-profile

We recommend that you use an interview guide to ensure that you thoroughly cover all seven areas. You can construct such a guide yourself, or alternatively, CEG Worldwide has put together an in-depth interview guide and scripts that we make available to advisors in our coaching programs.

We also recommend that you record your interview with a digital voice recorder. Let the prospect know that you will be recording the session so that you can stay fully engaged without worrying about missing some vital piece of information. You can also assure the prospect that whether or not he or she becomes your client, any recorded information will remain absolutely confidential. (Before making any recordings, be certain to get authorization from your compliance group and to find out the retention requirements for the recordings.)

As you ask questions in each area, do two things. First, listen—really deeply listen—to the prospect's responses, both so that he or she *feels heard* and so that you actually *have heard* what was said. In our hyper-sales-focused industry, far too many advisors are better at talking than at listening, but it's in the listening—the open and unhurried receiving of information—that a real relationship develops.

Second, create a mind map on an unlined piece of paper or flip chart. Begin by putting the prospect's name (or both names for a couple) in the center, and then draw connecting lines and text bubbles for each of the seven main areas of inquiry. As you move through your questions, capture the prospect's responses in the appropriate places, using any kind of graphic elements you like, not just words. Connect responses with lines when they relate to one another to illustrate the interconnectedness of the various parts of the prospect's life. Done well, a mind map will stimulate thorough responses, trigger new and deeper questions, and capture relevant information that randomly arises. **Exhibit 4.6** provides an example of a completed Total Client Profile. You may download a PDF of the sample Total Client Profile at www.cegworldwide.com/downloads/bt-book/eb_ceg_sample_tcp.pdf

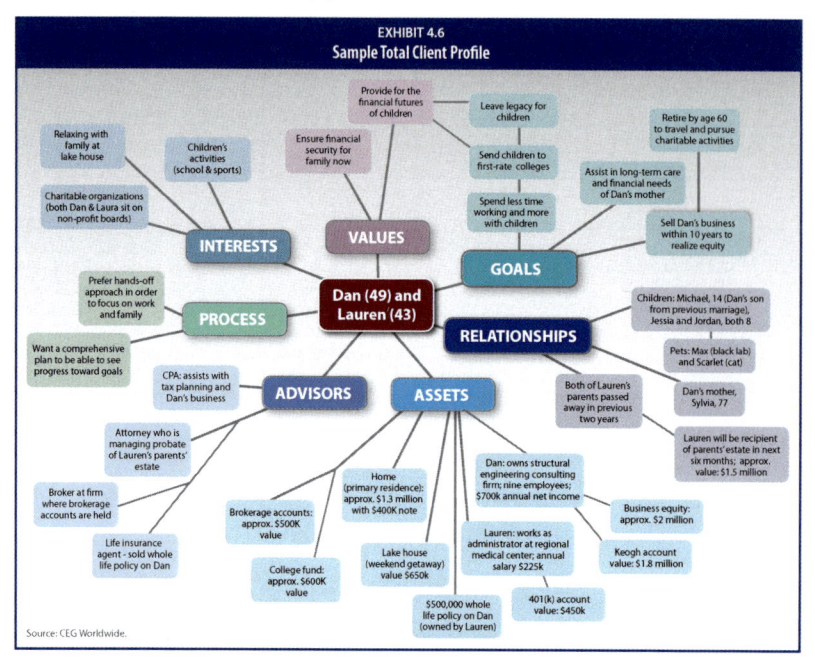

EXHIBIT 4.6
Sample Total Client Profile

A mind map centered on "Dan (49) and Lauren (43)" with branches for INTERESTS, VALUES, GOALS, RELATIONSHIPS, ASSETS, ADVISORS, and PROCESS.

- INTERESTS: Relaxing with family at lake house; Children's activities (school & sports); Charitable organizations (both Dan & Laura sit on non-profit boards)
- VALUES: Provide for the financial futures of children; Ensure financial security for family now
- GOALS: Leave legacy for children; Send children to first-rate colleges; Spend less time working and more with children; Assist in long-term care and financial needs of Dan's mother; Retire by age 60 to travel and pursue charitable activities; Sell Dan's business within 10 years to realize equity
- RELATIONSHIPS: Children: Michael, 14 (Dan's son from previous marriage), Jessia and Jordan, both 8; Pets: Max (black lab) and Scarlet (cat); Dan's mother, Sylvia, 77; Both of Lauren's parents passed away in previous two years; Lauren will be recipient of parents' estate in next six months; approx. value: $1.5 million
- ASSETS: Home (primary residence); approx. $1.3 million with $400K note; Brokerage accounts: approx. $500K value; College fund: approx. $600K value; Lake house (weekend getaway) value $650k; $500,000 whole life policy on Dan (owned by Lauren); Dan: owns structural engineering consulting firm; nine employees; $700k annual net income; Lauren: works as administrator at regional medical center; annual salary $225k; 401(k) account value: $450k; Keogh account value: $1.8 million; Business equity: approx. $2 million
- ADVISORS: CPA: assists with tax planning and Dan's business; Attorney who is managing probate of Lauren's parents' estate; Broker at firm where brokerage accounts are held; Life insurance agent - sold whole life policy on Dan
- PROCESS: Prefer hands-off approach in order to focus on work and family; Want a comprehensive plan to be able to see progress toward goals

Source: CEG Worldwide.

There are many advantages to using mind mapping over traditional note taking:

- It helps you drill down to the prospect's key issues faster and more accurately.

- It captures information quickly, yet in a highly organized format.

- It makes it easy to link and cross-reference very different, yet connected, pieces of the prospect's financial picture.

- It involves prospective clients more deeply in the discovery process, motivating them to provide you with all the information you need to complete their profiles.

- It provides a basis for moving forward with clear goals and next steps.

- It provides you with a document that is fast and easy to review.

- It is an excellent starting point for brainstorming solutions with members of your network of professional advisors.

The information you gather during the mind-mapping process will tell you whether the prospect fits your ideal client profile. If you discover that there is not a good match, then inform the prospect and move on. If it is a good match, then you will have all the information needed to move to the next step: creating an investment plan and a wealth management plan.

CCM2: Investment Plan Meeting

The Investment Plan Meeting should take place about two weeks after the Discovery Meeting. Here, you will present a detailed, actionable investment plan (along with an investment policy statement, or IPS) that will serve as a road map that maximizes the probability of achieving everything that's financially important to the prospect. It will also further establish you as an expert in the eyes of the prospect. During this meeting, you will also continue to build your personal relationship with the prospect.

Your primary task in advance of the Investment Plan Meeting is to create the prospect's investment plan. A well-designed investment plan serves the following important purposes:

- **It provides you with an opportunity to clarify and solidify the prospect's goals.** Drawn from the information gathered during the Discovery Meeting, the investment plan documents all seven areas from the prospect's Total Client Profile. Often the most critical area for investment decisions concerns the prospect's financial goals. By putting these goals in writing, the investment plan ensures that both you and the prospect are completely clear about this vital area.

- **It provides long-term discipline for the prospect's investment decision-making.** A well-drafted plan helps ensure that rational analysis is the basis for the prospect's investment decisions, making the prospect less likely to act on emotional responses to short-term or one-time events.

- **It promotes clear communication.** Because it clarifies the issues that are most important to the prospect and the approaches that you will use, the investment plan can prevent misunderstandings that might otherwise arise.

- **It provides you with an opportunity to "WOW" the prospect.** The investment plan demonstrates that you are extremely thoughtful in your approach to solving the prospect's financial challenges. The document reflects your thorough preparation, systematic strategy and close attention to detail.

Note that you are creating an *investment* plan here, not a *financial* plan. It's true that astute financial planning can play a crucial role in the overall wealth management process, which is why you will work with your professional network to create an advanced plan later on in the consultative process. But most advisors, especially at this early stage, find it extremely difficult to execute a financial plan either well or profitably. By positioning yourself as a financial planner, you are effectively communicating to prospective clients that you are an expert in all aspects of financial services, and this is simply impossible.

In contrast, an actionable, comprehensive investment plan communicates a very different message: that you are primarily focused on the one aspect of their finances that many affluent prospective clients are most concerned about—preserving their wealth. Only after the investment plan is in place will you turn your attention to the other major financial concerns, and you will do this in concert with experts in those other areas.

The investment plan itself should be divided into two parts:

1. **An executive summary of your investment consulting work and recommendations for the prospect.** This will provide an overview of the prospect's Total Client Profile, your consulting process and your investment recommendations. It should also include brief descriptions of your fees, as well as your firm's background and investment philosophy.

2. **An investment policy statement.** The IPS should delve into substantial detail as to your investing approach and strategic portfolio management process, thereby demonstrating to the prospective client the thoughtfulness of your firm's overall investment process. It should also provide summaries of the returns of key indexes and of a range of hypothetical portfolios that your firm recommends (rather than addressing the prospective client's individual situation).

There's no need to walk the prospect through the IPS in detail. Most high-net-worth personality types—with the exception of the Accumulator, the Gambler and the Innovator (who make the worst clients for wealth managers—see Chapter 3)—won't be interested in the details of your IPS. But all your clients will be glad that you do in fact have an IPS. (You should review your IPS on an annual basis to make any necessary changes and make sure that it addresses all regulatory requirements.)

As shown following, the mechanics of the Investment Plan Meeting are similar to those of the Discovery Meeting, from how you greet the prospect and cover the agenda to how you wrap up the meeting. The core of the meeting, of course, is presenting the investment plan. Go through it in detail and respond to any questions or concerns.

After you discuss the investment plan, ask the prospect for a commitment to move forward. You are not, at this point, looking to have the client actually invest—to actually write a check. Remember, you are using a consultative approach. It is not your job to persuade the prospect to do something, but to help the prospect understand what the right thing to do is. Then, as the prospect-turned-client's personal chief financial officer, your job is to execute the plan. So you want the prospect to take the time to really think things through. Many prospective clients are ready to invest at this second meeting, but you should insist that they take the materials back home and then return for a Mutual Commitment Meeting. At that point, if they are committed to achieving their goals vis-à-vis the investment plan, you will commit to their success where both parties can make the necessary commitment and execute the required paperwork.

Overview of Investment Plan Meeting Steps

1. Greet the prospect by name. Reinforce some aspect of his or her high-net-worth personality.
2. Set the stage for the meeting.
3. Outline the agenda and describe the remaining steps of the Consultative Client Management Process.
4. Walk the prospect through the investment plan.
5. Solicit and address concerns about the plan.
6. Ask for a commitment for moving forward.
7. Set the stage for the advanced plan.
8. Close the meeting.
9. Send confirmation of the next meeting.

After you have received the commitment, set the stage for the advanced plan. Explain that investments are only the foundation of the entire financial picture and that once the prospect becomes a client you will work with your network of professionals to identify those areas beyond investments where additional work may be needed.

> **WATCH THE VIDEO** ▶ **The Investment Plan Meeting**
> With Paul Brunswick
> www.cegworldwide.com/btbook/investment-plan-meeting

CCM3: Mutual Commitment Meeting

Schedule the Mutual Commitment Meeting about one week after the Investment Plan Meeting. At this meeting the prospect will ideally become a client.

This meeting has two objectives. The first is to make the mutual commitment to work together to achieve the client's goals and values. In addition to verbally ascertaining this, you will assist the client in executing the documents necessary to implement the investment plan. The second objective is to seek introductions to qualified prospects.

To get ready for the Mutual Commitment Meeting, prepare the paperwork necessary to execute the investment plan's recommendations. Review the investment plan and have a copy available for the meeting. Also review the client's entire file, including the Total Client Profile and your notes of any questions or concerns raised during the Investment Plan Meeting. Ensure that you are completely up to speed on the prospect's situation and investment plan so you can confidently and competently answer any further questions. And, of course, as with all meetings, prepare an agenda.

After greeting the prospect, collect and address any questions. After this, let the prospect know that you are excited about the progress you're making together and ask whether he or she is ready to move forward, become your client and set the investment plan in motion. To expedite the process, have all the paperwork prepared with "sign here" stickers attached in appropriate places. Take the time needed to explain all paperwork. This is also when you will collect any checks, as appropriate.

Once all the documents have been executed, pause for a moment to congratulate the client. Say something like this:

> "You should be commended for doing a great job. Congratulations on taking an extremely important step toward securing your financial future and achieving all the things that are important to you."

Explain to your client that some "buyer's remorse" is not uncommon at this point, especially if he or she is used to relying on the financial media for investment information and perspectives. Encourage your new client to ignore the financial media, if possible, or to view it merely as entertainment. Instead, the client should focus on making wise financial decisions—such as working with you—and sticking with a long-term plan for achieving all that is important in his or her financial life.

You may also want to talk to your new client a bit about the concentrated nature of investment gains. Explain that it will be easier to stay the course over the long run if he or she understands that the uneven nature of investment gains is an unavoidable part of attaining investment goals. Missing even short periods can result in dramatically lower returns over time than staying consistently invested all the time. Let the client know to expect down periods as well as up periods and that worrying about every little rise and dip will only lead to making the kind of mistakes that it's your job to help avoid.

Now that your prospect is a client, you should also begin to leverage the relationship by asking for introductions to friends, family members and colleagues who are qualified for your service. Since your new client is impressed enough to trust you with his or her financial future, the client is usually quite willing to help by introducing you to qualified prospects—you simply have to frame it as a second-opinion offer. Since introductions from your clients can be an extremely powerful tool for growing your business, we will go into considerable detail on exactly how to make the second-opinion offer in the next chapter.

As you close the meeting, explain that the 45-Day Follow-up Meeting is next. Schedule it about six weeks out. One of the main objectives of that meeting will be to help the new client get organized, so ask the client to save all paperwork and bring it to the meeting. Reassure the client that even if some of the paperwork seems confusing or overwhelming, you and your staff will certainly help with all of it. Then close the meeting by acknowledging that you are glad that you can play an important role in helping your client achieve all that is important to him or her.

Overview of Mutual Commitment Meeting Steps

1. Greet the prospect by name. Reinforce some aspect of his or her high-net-worth personality.
2. Collect all questions and then address them.
3. Execute the documents.
4. Congratulate the client.
5. Caution the client about "buyer's remorse."
6. Explain the concentrated nature of investment gains.
7. Make the second-opinion service offer.
8. Close the meeting.
9. Send confirmation of the next meeting.

WATCH THE VIDEO ▶ **The Mutual Commitment Meeting**
With Paul Brunswick
www.cegworldwide.com/btbook/mutual-commit-meeting

CCM4: 45-Day Follow-up Meeting

So much paperwork is generated when money is transferred, especially when multiple accounts are involved, that it's quite easy for your client to become inundated in the weeks following the investment plan's implementation. The 45-Day Follow-up Meeting allows you to help the client understand and organize all this financial paperwork. At the same time, it provides you with an opportunity to impress your new client with the quality of your service and gives you a second opportunity to request introductions to qualified prospects.

To prepare for the meeting, create a tabbed notebook with sections for the investment plan overview, the investment policy statement, the advanced plan, brokerage statements, your regular progress reports, your newsletter (if you produce one) and miscellaneous communications. Emphasize the long-term nature of your relationship by designing the notebook to accommodate a minimum of five years' worth of paperwork. Alternately, if your client prefers, you can create an online storage area for electronic copies of all the paperwork.

After you greet the client and settle down, begin by gathering and responding to any questions. Find out whether there have been changes in the client's life, such as a job change, a divorce, or a recent birth or death in the family—all of which can require adjustments to the wealth management plan. Simply ask: "Has anything changed personally, professionally or financially since we last met?"

Next, give the client the notebook that you prepared in advance and briefly explain what each tabbed section in the notebook is for. Place all the documents in the appropriate sections, showing the client how to read and understand each document. If the client prefers a virtual version of the notebook, show him or her how to access and view the records electronically.

Many portfolio management software programs annualize returns even for short periods, and your client will no doubt notice these returns as you are helping to organize the paperwork. If the market did well during the 45 days since the client began working with you, the annualization of the returns will make you look like a genius. On the other hand, if the market is down, the negative returns will make the client wonder why he or she is paying you.

We recommend that you turn this into a learning opportunity, using it as a real-world illustration of the irrelevancy of short-term returns. Explain it like this:

> "What's really important is not investment performance over any isolated period, but achieving your goals over your lifetime. What has happened in the last 45 days has little to do with achieving your goals, because in the long run, the only way to achieve your goals is to make smart decisions about your money. In the short term, no one can know with any accuracy how the market will move. But in the long term, by making prudent decisions, we can maximize the probability of your success."

Before closing the meeting, make the second-opinion offer, as you did in the Mutual Commitment Meeting. Then schedule the first Regular Progress Meeting. We recommend that these meetings take place on a systematic basis based on the preference the client indicated during your discussion of process during the Discovery Meeting. Confirm the client's preference, and schedule appropriately.

> ### Overview of 45-Day Follow-up Meeting Steps
>
> 1. Greet the client by name. Reinforce some aspect of his or her high-net-worth personality.
> 2. Gather and respond to questions.
> 3. Ask about changes in the client's life.
> 4. Organize the paperwork.
> 5. Place short-term progress into a long-term perspective.
> 6. Make the second-opinion service offer.
> 7. Schedule the next meeting.
> 8. Send confirmation of the next meeting.

WATCH THE VIDEO ▶ **The 45-Day Follow-up Meeting**
With Paul Brunswick
www.cegworldwide.com/btbook/45-day-follow-up

CCM5: Regular Progress Meetings

Regular Progress Meetings give you an opportunity to do three things. First, they let you review your client's progress toward meeting his or her goals. You can answer any questions your client has and help put his or her mind at ease, especially during difficult market climates.

Second, these meetings allow you to continue to build and deepen the client-advisor relationship. You can stay on top of what's happening in your client's life, and you can also continue to gather introductions to qualified prospects as well as additional assets. Ultimately, you want to build such a close relationship and do such a good job for all your clients that they become your marketing apostles.

Third, these meetings give you the opportunity to present and then execute an advanced plan. The plan will contain a range of recommendations designed to meet specific financial challenges, each prioritized according to the impact it can have on the client's life. Crafted well, the advanced plan will enable you to deal with each area systematically while maintaining an integrated approach to the client's overall financial picture.

In the first Regular Progress Meeting you will present your client with the advanced plan. In most cases you will rely on your professional network of advisors, described later in this chapter, to analyze your client's situation and make the appropriate recommendations. Every advanced plan should deal with the four key areas of the client's financial life beyond his or her investments that we have discussed:

1. **Wealth enhancement:** producing the best possible investment returns consistent with the client's level of risk tolerance while minimizing the tax impact on those returns.

2. **Wealth transfer:** facilitating the most tax-efficient way to pass assets to succeeding generations in a way that meets the client's wishes.

3. **Wealth protection:** protecting the client's wealth against potential creditors, litigants, children's spouses and potential ex-spouses, as well as protecting the client against catastrophic loss.

4. **Charitable giving:** fulfilling the client's charitable goals, which can often support efforts in each of the other three areas.

The mechanics of the Regular Progress Meetings are straightforward. Walk through your agenda and then ask the client whether he or she has any items or questions to add to it. Since your progress report will probably answer most of your client's questions, refrain from immediately answering any questions or concerns at this time. Next, inquire about any major changes in the client's personal or financial life, just as you did at the beginning of the 45-Day Follow-up Meeting. Ask clarifying follow-up questions if needed, and note the changes on the client's Total Client Profile.

Now go over the client's current investment position, pointing out any significant changes. Review progress for the quarter, year to date and since inception. Explain performance, placing it within the context of the appropriate market benchmarks. Also discuss any changes that you anticipate making. Frame all of this within the larger context of whether or not the client is on track to achieving all his or her most important financial goals.

> **Overview of the First Regular Progress Meeting**
> 1. Greet the client by name. Reinforce some aspect of his or her high-net-worth personality.
> 2. Review the agenda.
> 3. Collect questions.
> 4. Ask about major changes in the client's life.
> 5. Review investment performance.
> 6. Present the advanced plan.
> 7. Discuss and prioritize action items in the advanced plan.
> 8. Answer any additional questions.
> 9. Make the second-opinion service offer.
> 10. Request additional assets to manage.
> 11. Schedule the next Regular Progress Meeting.
> 12. Send out confirmation of the next meeting.

Once you have moved through the whole plan, discuss each recommended action, providing as much detail as the client needs to make a decision about moving forward on that item. Your job here is to help coach the client to make one of three choices with respect to each recommendation: drop it, defer it or do it. Take notes on the client's decisions on each item and assign a priority to each task the client decides to undertake. Answer any remaining questions.

You will next make the second-opinion offer, as in previous meetings. In addition, you will request additional assets to manage—something you

> **Critical Success Factors for Regular Progress Meetings**
>
> - **Be prepared.** You need to know exactly what's going on with the investment account as well as with any current activity related to implementing recommendations from the advanced plan. If there have been any major changes since your last meeting, notify the client in advance so that there are no surprises.
>
> - **Have timely information.** Always use the most up-to-date information possible—the previous day's closing statements.
>
> - **Reinforce the long-term perspective.** Remind the client of the importance of maintaining a long-term perspective to stay on track and achieve important goals, even when short-term investment performance is down.
>
> - **Keep your edge.** It's easy to fall into the trap of routine when conducting Regular Progress Meetings. You owe it to your client to deliver a world-class experience every time.

will learn how to do in the next chapter. Wrap up by scheduling the next Regular Progress Meeting.

Subsequent Regular Progress Meetings will follow the same agenda, with several differences. Review progress for both the investment plan and the advanced plan. Educate the client on particularly relevant aspects of each plan, making sure that high-priority items remain prominent in your client's mind. If a complex wealth management solution—such as a family limited partnership—is on the table, it can be very helpful to bring in the appropriate expert from your professional network to discuss the issue directly with the client.

Building Your Professional Network

By combining the Consultative Client Management Process with your investment management skills, you will be fully positioned to meet the investment needs of your affluent clients. But to be a successful wealth manager, you need to address the totality of your clients' financial challenges with the best possible strategies, services and products. This is something that you can't do alone, because no one person can be an expert in the entire range of advanced planning needs and solutions. Instead, you will build a network of professionals, experts who have deep knowledge in the four advanced planning specialties.

Exhibit 4.7 shows a sample professional network. The network that you create will in part depend on your target affluent niche, since different types of affluent clients have different needs. At a minimum, though, your professional network should be composed of four core team members: you as wealth manager, a private client lawyer, an accountant and a life insurance specialist.

**EXHIBIT 4.7
A Sample Professional Network**

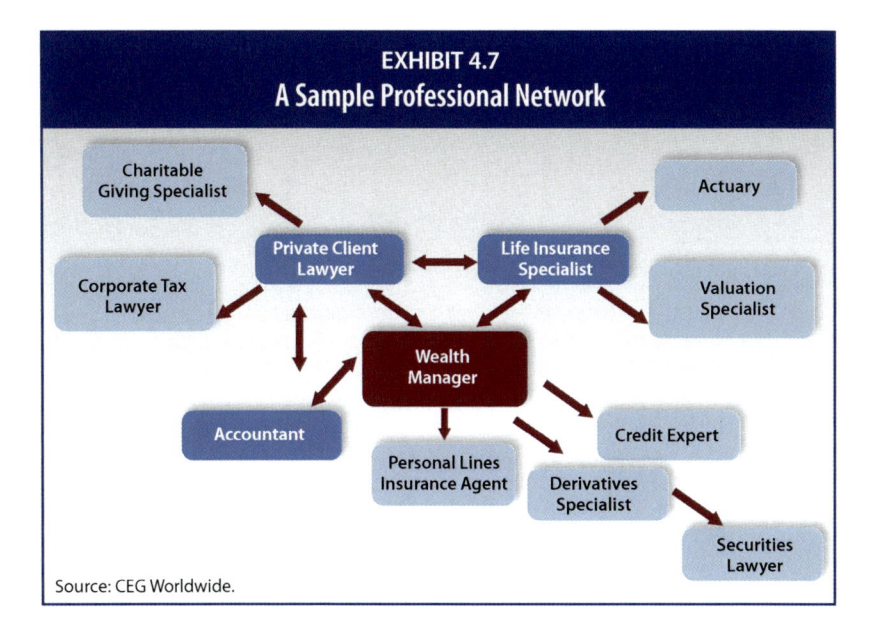

Source: CEG Worldwide.

- **The wealth manager.** As the wealth manager, you have three primary roles with respect to your professional network:

    1. To build the network and manage it on an ongoing basis

    2. To provide the network members with a deep understanding of each client

    3. To facilitate the network meetings to draw out the optimal recommendations for your clients

- **The private client lawyer.** The private client lawyer is the key member of the professional network. He or she addresses tax, estate planning and legal needs—all critical areas of concern for solving the challenges of wealthy clients.

- **The accountant.** While the private client lawyer will provide a big-picture perspective on tax planning, the accountant typically has much more detailed, day-to-day knowledge of income taxes. He or she should be able to make specific recommendations to mitigate these taxes.

- **The life insurance specialist.** The insurance specialist works closely with the private client lawyer to identify and structure solutions that leverage the entire range of life insurance products. You want a true independent—not someone who receives any kind of incentive from a company. In addition, to avoid any potential for conflict, this specialist should not offer investments.

Other specialists in your network might include a personal lines insurance specialist (a property-casualty agent who works at the very high end of the market); a credit expert to advise on loans; a corporate tax lawyer, especially for clients with fast-growing businesses; a derivatives specialist, who deals with concentrated tax positions; a securities lawyer, who supports the work of the derivatives specialist; an income tax specialist, for truly complex tax situations; an actuary, to support the work of the insurance specialist; and a valuation specialist, for appraising business interests, real estate or collectibles. There are many other experts who may need to be part of your network, depending on the general needs of members of your target niche and the specific needs of your actual clients.

You don't necessarily need to establish a close relationship with every expert in your network. Instead, rely on your core team members—the private client lawyer, accountant and life insurance specialist—to bring in their own experts as needed. But you do need to carefully select these three core team members. The members of your professional network must embody four key traits: specific expertise, integrity, professionalism and chemistry. Finding the right individuals will take some time and effort, so make sure you start this process early on. (Unfortunately, size constraints necessarily limit this book's discussion of selecting, vetting and managing your team of experts. CEG Worldwide's coaching programs, however, include a detailed and systematic approach to locating and choosing experts.)

> **Compensation for the Wealth Manager**
>
> As the wealth manager, the client is yours. You should therefore expect to receive a portion of each professional's fee. (One clear exception is legal fees. In every case, your client hires the lawyer directly and you will receive no portion of his or her fees.)
>
> Your compensation will vary according to the professionals you work with. Generally speaking, for insurance products, you can expect a fifty-fifty split of commissions (which are typically 90 percent to 120 percent of the first year's premium). For credit, you can expect a finder's fee or points. You should also get a portion of the commissions on derivatives transactions.
>
> When you provide the client with investment management services yourself, you can (and should) charge a premium fee for these services, as compensation for providing all the other wealth management services. And when you execute strategies that have no products involved (for example, tax arbitrage between different countries), you can charge a project execution fee.
>
> Obviously, all fees should be fully disclosed and transparent to your client. In addition, you should work with your compliance group to make sure you are properly licensed before moving forward.

WATCH THE VIDEO ▶ **Build Your Expert Team**
With John Bowen
www.cegworldwide.com/btbook/build-expert-team

Uncovering Wealth Management Opportunities at the Professional Network Meeting

Once your professional network is complete (or you at least have in place the three key players: the private client lawyer, accountant and life insurance specialist), schedule a series of quarterly professional network meetings. (Depending on the number of affluent clients you have, in some cases you may want to get together with your experts as frequently as monthly.) If your professionals are located nearby, you should conduct these meetings in person, but telephone conferences work nearly as well after a business relationship is established. Set an agenda for each meeting and circulate it in advance.

Your main goal for these meetings is to identify, prioritize and document all opportunities for assisting each client in each advanced planning area. Begin by presenting the first client's Total Client Profile. (Remove all identifying information to maintain confidentiality.) Network members, especially new ones, may ask for additional details and financial documents, so remind them that this is a strategic, high-level conversation and that all you are asking for at this point is help on determining next steps for the client.

Following the presentation, facilitate brainstorming on the case by inviting recommendations in each of the four advanced planning areas. Capture ideas on a whiteboard, using the same mind-mapping technique you use for creating clients' Total Client Profiles. Then prioritize: Determine which actions should be taken first to make the greatest possible positive impact on achieving the client's key goals while ensuring your profitability.

Repeat this process for up to six client cases.

Drawing on the information and insights you gained during the brainstorming process, document the opportunities for actions that will address the client's needs. To do so, we recommend that you develop an advanced planning mind map. **Exhibit 4.8** provides an example of how such a mind map can be used to track the various activities involved in the four elements of advanced planning. You may download a PDF of the advanced planning mind map at www.cegworldwide.com/downloads/bt-book/eb_ceg_ap_map.pdf.

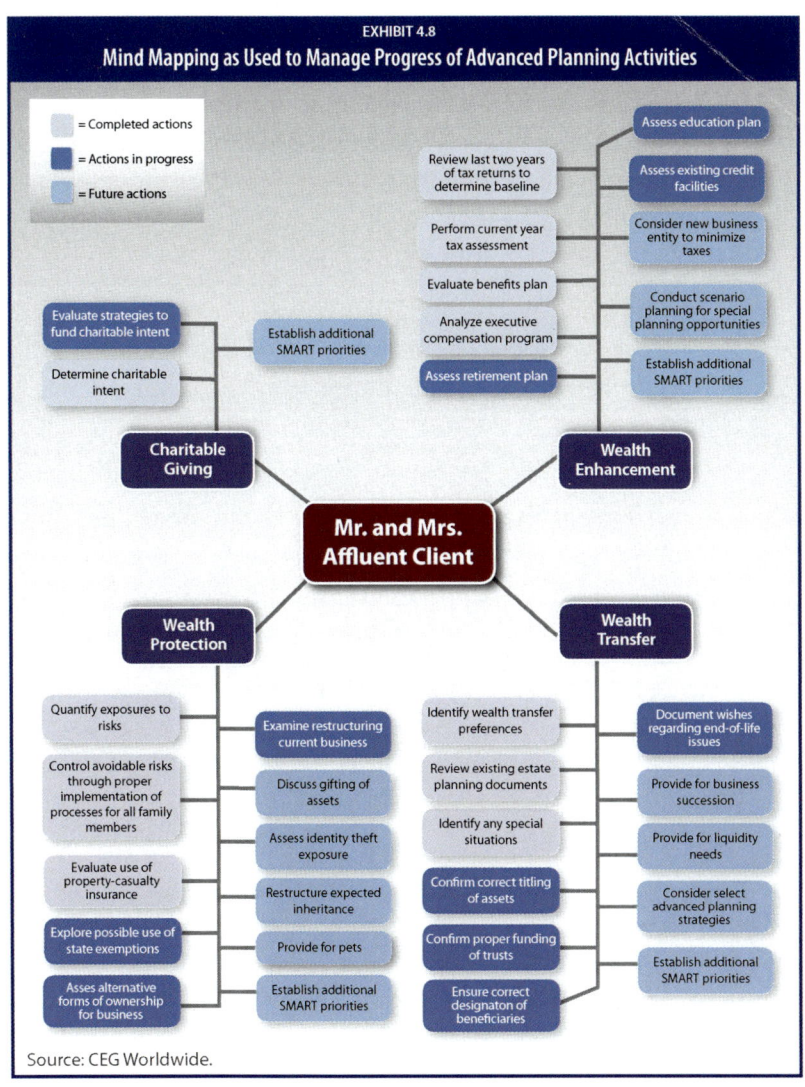

EXHIBIT 4.8
Mind Mapping as Used to Manage Progress of Advanced Planning Activities

- = Completed actions
- = Actions in progress
- = Future actions

Mr. and Mrs. Affluent Client

Charitable Giving
- Evaluate strategies to fund charitable intent
- Determine charitable intent
- Establish additional SMART priorities

Wealth Enhancement
- Review last two years of tax returns to determine baseline
- Perform current year tax assessment
- Evaluate benefits plan
- Analyze executive compensation program
- Assess retirement plan
- Assess education plan
- Assess existing credit facilities
- Consider new business entity to minimize taxes
- Conduct scenario planning for special planning opportunities
- Establish additional SMART priorities

Wealth Protection
- Quantify exposures to risks
- Control avoidable risks through proper implementation of processes for all family members
- Evaluate use of property-casualty insurance
- Explore possible use of state exemptions
- Asses alternative forms of ownership for business
- Examine restructuring current business
- Discuss gifting of assets
- Assess identity theft exposure
- Restructure expected inheritance
- Provide for pets
- Establish additional SMART priorities

Wealth Transfer
- Identify wealth transfer preferences
- Review existing estate planning documents
- Identify any special situations
- Confirm correct titling of assets
- Confirm proper funding of trusts
- Ensure correct designaton of beneficiaries
- Document wishes regarding end-of-life issues
- Provide for business succession
- Provide for liquidity needs
- Consider select advanced planning strategies
- Establish additional SMART priorities

Source: CEG Worldwide.

Keeping the Network Running Well

Bringing together a group of top professionals is one thing; getting them to work together as a smoothly functioning and effective team is quite another. These actions will help you get top performance from your network:

- **Establish a common vision.** You should be able not only to paint a picture for members of your network of what you all—together—are trying to accomplish, but also to achieve consensus around that vision. Your vision should include the comprehensive and client-centered wealth management you will provide, the satisfaction of working with other top-tier experts, and the resulting financial rewards.

- **Agree on who's in charge.** The network will run smoothly only when members understand their roles. In particular, it must be clear that the clients are yours and that you are ultimately the one responsible for making decisions about what's best for them.

- **Formalize how and when members of the network will communicate.** Set up clear processes and timetables for meeting and collaborating. This is particularly important in a virtual network, where face-to-face contact is at a premium.

- **Seek to continually improve your professional network meetings.** These sessions are when most group "bonding" will take place. Solicit feedback to help enhance your processes, your facilitation skills and the recommendations you provide to clients.

- **Keep them motivated.** Finally, keep in mind the old adage that nothing succeeds like success. The members of your professional network will be happy and motivated when they see the success of the team translated into income for them.

This mind map will contain recommended actions and document the order of priority of each action, as determined by you and the members of your network. It therefore enables you and your client to easily see the "big picture"—all activities are on a single page, and each is coded as to its status (already completed, in progress or slated for the future). Many advisors find that such mind maps are highly effective at guiding their work and focusing the discussion through each of the Regular Progress Meetings.

This chapter has covered a lot of ground. But once you have moved ten or 20 clients through the entire consultative process, you will find that not only are you better at delivering wealth management than you ever imagined you would be, but also that these clients are very enthusiastic about working with you. As a result, they will be highly inclined to give you more of their assets to manage and to introduce you to qualified prospects. Let's now turn, then, to exactly how to gain additional assets from existing clients and how to bring in new ideal clients.

Chapter 5
Capture Assets and Acquire Clients

WITH THE RIGHT CLIENTS IN HAND AND THE RIGHT business model in place to serve them, it's time to focus on surefire business development processes that will bring you ever-increasing financial rewards. These are the three surest paths to growing your business:

- Capture additional assets from existing clients.
- Formalize your client introductions program.
- Form strategic alliances with attorneys and accountants.

In this chapter, we'll take a close look at each approach.

Capture Additional Assets from Existing Clients

You should use the consultative wealth management process not just with prospective clients, but with your existing clients as well. In fact, once you have determined which—if any—of your existing clients fit your ideal client profile, immediately implement the consultative process with them. Start with the Discovery Meeting (which, with existing clients, we call a "rediscovery" meeting).

Since they already trust you, working with these clients provides you with an ideal opportunity to refine your new consultative skills and process. Better served by your new wealth management process, these clients will be predisposed to give you more of their assets to manage and to introduce you to friends and colleagues whom you could serve well.

We will even go so far as to say that if you have a sufficient number of existing ideal clients, you should not undertake any new business development efforts until you have completed at least ten rediscovery meetings. If you are like most financial advisors we've worked with, you will find that your current clients represent a gold mine of additional business, there for the asking.

How can this be? While many advisors believe that most of their clients do not have other financial advisors, the data show that this simply is not true, especially with respect to the affluent. Yes, most (86.1 percent) clients with $500,000 to $1 million of investable assets have only one advisor, but for those with $1 million to $2 million of investable assets, only 26.4 percent have only one advisor, and for those with $2 million to $6 million of investable assets, only 2.5 percent have just a single advisor. **(See Exhibit 5.1.)**

EXHIBIT 5.1
Number of Financial Advisors

Number of Advisors	$500,000–$1 million	$1 million–$2 million	$2 million–$6 million	Total
One	86.1%	26.4%	2.5%	42.1%
Two	12.6%	61.3%	56.0%	43.7%
Three or more	1.3%	12.3%	41.5%	14.2%

N = 1,417 individuals.
Source: Russ Alan Prince and David A. Geracioti, *Cultivating the Middle-Class Millionaire*, 2005.

Many wealthier individuals prefer to have their money invested with more than one financial advisor. In a sense, affluent people view having multiple advisors as a form of diversification. By spreading their money around, the wealthy feel that they can improve their overall investment returns, as well as the odds of finding at least one advisor who is really on top of things overall, someone who can reliably provide the services and solutions that they need and want.

There is considerable good news and (perhaps) some bad news here. If you have a compelling value proposition that sets you apart from other financial advisors—which your consultative wealth management process gives you—there's a good chance you can gain the business of prospective affluent ideal clients even when they already have other advisors.

Another piece of good news is that your existing affluent clients more than likely have assets in place with one or more other advisors (or simply sitting in a money market account, deposited in a CD or tucked under the proverbial mattress). The consultative process offers you numerous opportunities to ask your affluent clients about such assets. Once you uncover these assets, you can offer a second opinion on how they are being managed. You can also simply ask your clients if they would like you to manage these other assets going forward. As you consistently delight and even thrill your clients with a top-notch client experience, they in turn will be inclined to offer you even more of their assets to manage.

More good news: You can ignore the many self-appointed industry gurus who say you should work with clients only when you have all their assets. This contention simply ignores the reality shown in **Exhibit 5.1**.

Now for the "bad" news—which really isn't all that bad if you see it as an opportunity. Whether you gain a new ideal client or are working with an existing one, that client, especially if he or she is very wealthy, is predisposed to placing some of his or her money with another advisor. And that's exactly why it's so important for you to differentiate yourself from other advisors through the consultative wealth management process.

One last piece of good news: Notwithstanding what **Exhibit 5.1** shows us, we believe that most clients, even the most-affluent ones, would prefer to have a single close relationship with a trusted financial advisor capable of meeting almost all their financial needs. Turn yourself into this trusted, capable advisor, and both additional assets and referrals will come your way from your affluent clients.

The Process for (and Secret to) Capturing More Assets

It's far easier to grow your business by gathering additional assets from existing clients than by the expensive, time-consuming route of prospecting for new clients. But there's a secret to capturing additional assets from existing clients, one that's a key part of our proven five-step process:

Step 1. Set Expectations

Keeping in mind that each of your affluent clients probably has multiple advisors, your goal is to increase your share of your clients' assets by ensuring that they are completely satisfied with their relationship with you. Set expectations by reminding your clients at each of your Regular Progress Meetings that you are keenly interested in their overall well-being, which includes taking into account their overall asset allocation and the ways that any assets not placed with you are being managed.

Step 2. Review the Client Relationship

Periodically inquire as to what your clients do and do not like about their relationship with you. In addition to asking about this at your Regular Progress Meetings, conduct an annual client satisfaction survey. Remember, investment performance, which you can't completely control in any case, only goes so far in guaranteeing client satisfaction. What you can fully control is the quality of your client relationships and of the services you deliver. If a client is blasé about your relationship, only exceptional investment performance will garner additional assets. But if your relationship is exceptionally strong—something the consultative process facilitates—you are likely to gain additional assets even without exceptional investment performance.

Step 3. Identify Asset Transfer Opportunities

You must have a clear understanding of the overall assets of your clients—what they have and who's managing it. The consultative process provides you with this knowledge. Once you have completed a Discovery (or rediscovery) Meeting, you will know about the assets managed by other financial advisors and be able to target them for capture.

Step 4. Ask for Additional Assets

On occasion a very satisfied client may offer you additional assets without prompting. For the most part, however, you must ask for the additional assets.

Step 5. Thank Your Clients

Let your clients know that you appreciate the trust they've placed in you, whether or not you have received any additional assets. Always keep in mind that the relationships you have with your affluent clients are the ultimate key to your long-term success.

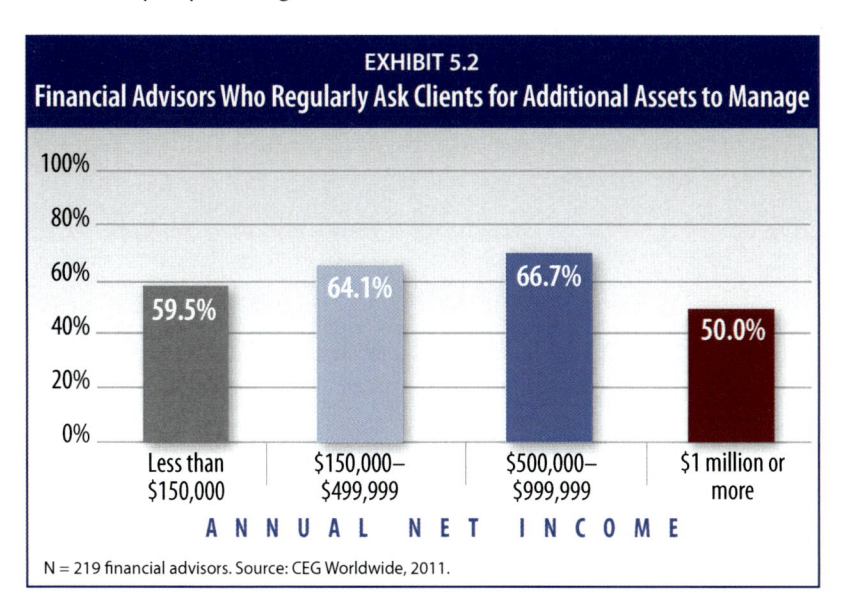

EXHIBIT 5.2
Financial Advisors Who Regularly Ask Clients for Additional Assets to Manage

Annual Net Income	Percentage
Less than $150,000	59.5%
$150,000–$499,999	64.1%
$500,000–$999,999	66.7%
$1 million or more	50.0%

N = 219 financial advisors. Source: CEG Worldwide, 2011.

What, then, is the secret to additional asset capture? It's Step 4: You actually have to ask. As **Exhibit 5.2** shows, financial advisors overall have great room for improvement here. Of the elite financial advisors we surveyed in 2011, fewer than two-thirds overall reported asking their clients for additional assets on a regular basis. And as you can see, this is one area where the high-income financial advisors do not excel—in fact, they request additional assets at a lower rate than less-successful advisors. It's simple: If you don't ask, you won't get—so go ahead and ask.

> ### Critical Success Factors for Asset Capture
>
> Many financial advisors feel uncomfortable asking for additional assets. Keeping these important points in mind will make it easier:
>
> - When you deliver a consistent, top-notch level of service and rely on a systematic consultative process, your clients are likely to be increasingly satisfied with you and have good reason to give you more assets.
>
> - As a result of your Discovery Meetings, you will already know what other assets your clients have. You will be able to specify exactly what you are asking for and why.
>
> - Ask for additional assets when your clients are most satisfied with you, for example, during your Regular Progress Meetings or after you have successfully provided an advanced planning solution.
>
> - Although it's theoretically possible that a client might be offended or otherwise put off by your asking for more assets, we've never heard of it happening.

WATCH THE VIDEO ▶ **Profile in Success: Gordon Bernhardt**
McLean, Virginia
www.cegworldwide.com/btbook/gordon-bernhardt

Formalize Your Client Introductions Program

There are two keys to obtaining qualified client introductions. The first is to have satisfied clients. Not only are satisfied clients more likely to stay with you, they are more likely to introduce you to the people they care about. They want to share with their friends and business associates their great experience of working with you (just like you want to tell people about the great book you just read or great massage therapist you just found). Through your wealth management process, you are well-equipped to serve your clients very well, build the long-term relationship they want and ensure their ongoing satisfaction.

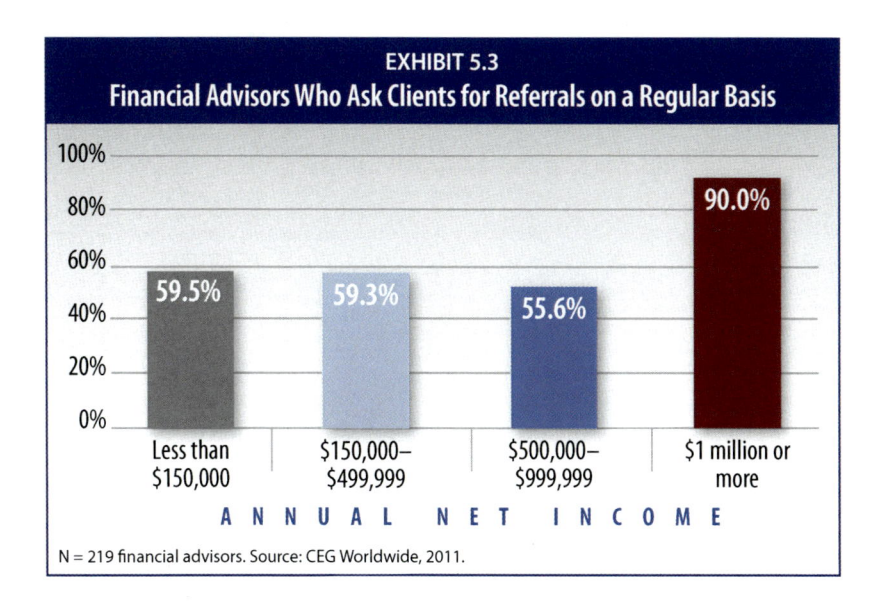

EXHIBIT 5.3
Financial Advisors Who Ask Clients for Referrals on a Regular Basis

Annual Net Income	Percentage
Less than $150,000	59.5%
$150,000–$499,999	59.3%
$500,000–$999,999	55.6%
$1 million or more	90.0%

N = 219 financial advisors. Source: CEG Worldwide, 2011.

The second key is to systematically ask for client introductions. You can't simply wait for your clients to introduce you to prospects. **Exhibit 5.3** tells us that the high-income advisors know this very well—nine out of ten of those earning at least $1 million a year ask their clients for introductions on a regular basis.

Exhibit 5.4 shows that asking for introductions on a regular basis works. The high-income financial advisors we surveyed received an average of 5.9 introductions from each of their top 20 clients over the previous year—far more than all other advisors received. This rate of introductions can lead to exceptional growth for your business and may be the only type of growth you need to cultivate.

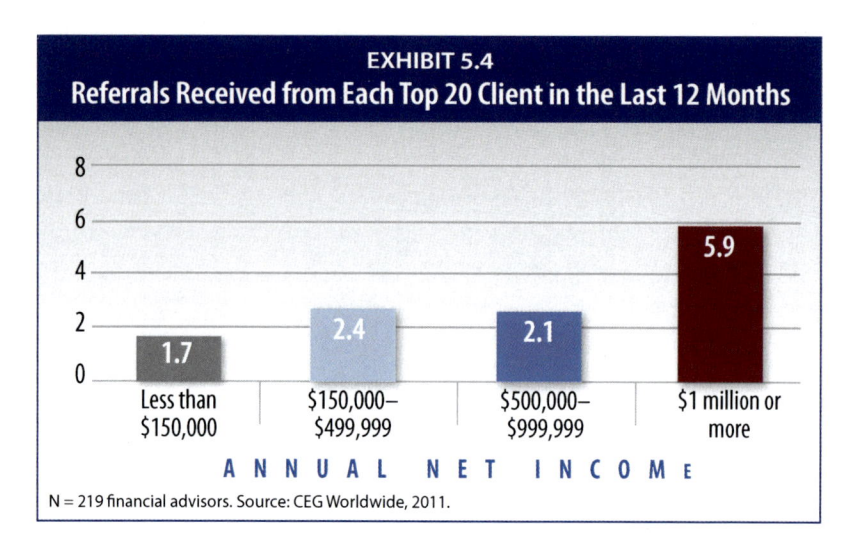

EXHIBIT 5.4
Referrals Received from Each Top 20 Client in the Last 12 Months

Annual Net Income	Referrals
Less than $150,000	1.7
$150,000–$499,999	2.4
$500,000–$999,999	2.1
$1 million or more	5.9

N = 219 financial advisors. Source: CEG Worldwide, 2011.

The 12-Step Client Introduction Request Process

A highly satisfied client may occasionally introduce you to a prospect without being prompted, but you can't count on a steady stream of such introductions. As our research shows, asking for introductions results in receiving introductions, so you must ask.

The key is to do so in a way that will make your clients highly likely to introduce you to qualified prospective clients. The 12-step process we recommend has proven to be one of the most effective business-building techniques for participants in our coaching programs.

Step 1. Make the Second-Opinion Service Offer

Some financial advisors shy away from asking their clients for introductions because they see it as asking their clients to do something that is of benefit only to the financial advisor, not to the clients themselves.

When you ask your clients for introductions—and frame the request in the way we recommend—you are offering to extend this gift to the people they care about. You are offering a service with not just a very high perceived value, but a very high actual value. Given this, you should feel absolutely comfortable and confident in making the offer.

Below is the script we recommend that you use to make the second-opinion service offer.

> "I wanted to offer you a service that we provide to our best clients for the people they care most about. With all the complexity and volatility in today's financial markets, many investors are actively considering switching financial advisors. They're unsure of what to do now. Are they well-positioned to stay with their current financial advisors or should they switch financial advisors? And if so, how can they find the right one?
>
> "To help these people that you care most about, we now offer our second-opinion service so that they can make informed decisions. In this service, we provide a second opinion. We take them through the same experience you had with our discovery process to get very clear on where they are now and where they'd like to go. We'll examine any of the gaps that need to be filled and if they're in good shape with their current providers, we'll let them know. Or if it's more appropriate for us to work with them, we'll begin that process.

"As you know, we work only with clients for whom we can have a major impact. If they should consider switching financial advisors and we're not a good fit, we'll be happy to point them in the right direction for a financial advisor who can work with them more effectively."

Step 2. Ask for the Introduction

Now pose this simple question: "Whom do you know who would most benefit from our second-opinion service?"

Step 3. Ask for Another Introduction

Once you have received a name, ask for another. Just say this: "Great! Who else comes to mind?" Continue to ask until no other prospect names are offered.

Step 4. Gather Contact Information

Once you have a list of names, ask for the background and contact information of each one, as well as what would be the best way to approach each.

Step 5. Ask for a Personal Introduction

In most cases, the most effective way to establish contact with the prospective clients is to have the client contact them to let them know that you will be getting in touch with them very soon. They can do this either by phone or email.

Step 6. Commit to Follow Up

Since your client is making the effort of contacting the people being introduced, assure him or her that you will follow up immediately.

Step 7. Wrap Up

Simply express your appreciation by saying, "I really appreciate your introductions and will look forward to providing them with a second opinion on their finances."

Step 8. Thank Your Client

You should quickly reciprocate by expressing your thanks in a handwritten note. This has become a lost art and is greatly appreciated. If you don't have good handwriting, have someone who does write the note for you. Failing that, you can send an email, but it is much less effective. Your personal handwritten note should ideally be sent out on the same day that you receive the introduction, and no later than the following day.

Step 9. Call Each Prospect

Your goal for the initial contact with each referral prospect should be to arrange a Discovery Meeting. The person will respond in one of three ways, each of which requires a different response from you.

1. **"No."** Prospective clients who decline to meet will typically do so because they already have a financial advisor. If this is the case, then inquire as to whether they would like a free second opinion on their finances.

2. **"Maybe."** You will seldom get this response, but when you do, it's most often because the prospect has hesitation about cost. If so, let the prospect know that there's no cost for an initial Discovery Meeting and that in any case you wouldn't take him or her on as a client unless you were sure you could add real value to his or her financial life.

3. **"Yes."** Schedule a date and time to get together. Explain that you will send a follow-up letter outlining the financial information and records you would like to have him or her bring to the meeting in order to make the meeting extremely productive.

> **Here are a few common mistakes that you can easily avoid:**
>
> - **Failing to ask.** As with capturing additional assets, if you don't ask, you don't get. So go ahead and ask. The worst that can happen is that your client says "no."
>
> - **Failing to follow through.** Follow through religiously on every introduction. Otherwise you not only waste your time and effort, you lose credibility with the client who provided the introduction. (Imagine how embarrassed your client will be if he or she mentions you to the prospect and finds out you never made contact.)
>
> - **Failing to stick with your ideal client profile.** Don't blindly pursue every prospect who comes your way. If the occasional prospect who doesn't precisely match your ideal client profile happens to have significant investable assets and you know you could easily add substantial value to him or her, it might make sense to take this individual as a client. But this is a judgment call. Remember that, for the most part, the more you are distracted from your core competencies, the less successful you will be.

Step 10. Send an Invitation to the Prospect

Immediately after arranging the Discovery Meeting, send a follow-up letter to prepare him or her for the meeting, as we discussed in Chapter 4.

Step 11. Let Your Client Know the Results

Your client will be curious about how things work out, so it's important that you inform him or her about what happened. (You do need to protect client confidentiality, of course, so get the prospect's permission to report back to the client who provided the introduction.) A quick note or an email is better than a phone call, but immediate feedback is desirable either way.

Step 12. Thank Each Client—Again

A client who provides one introduction is likely to provide introductions again. Keep the client inclined to make additional introductions by acknowledging how much you appreciate the client's assistance.

Some financial advisors like to thank their clients with small gifts, such as gift baskets. Others like to take the clients out to dinner, but we have found (not surprisingly) that most clients prefer dinner with their spouses to dinner with their financial advisors. This makes a gift certificate to a client's favorite restaurant a nice gift. Be sure to check with your compliance group on rules regarding gifts.

WATCH THE VIDEO — **Making Introductions Happen**
With John Bowen
www.cegworldwide.com/btbook/making-introductions

Form Strategic Alliances with Attorneys and Accountants

Developing strategic alliances with other professionals who are in a position to introduce you to ideal prospective clients is a great way to boost your long-term business growth. Consider that affluent individuals *want* to find their financial advisors through such referrals. **As Exhibit 5.5** shows, 54.2 percent of the affluent clients surveyed reported that a referral from an accountant or an attorney was an important way to find their primary financial advisors.

What exactly is a strategic alliance? In contrast to informal referral arrangements, a strategic alliance is an agreement that creates a vested

EXHIBIT 5.5
Importance in Finding Primary Financial Advisor

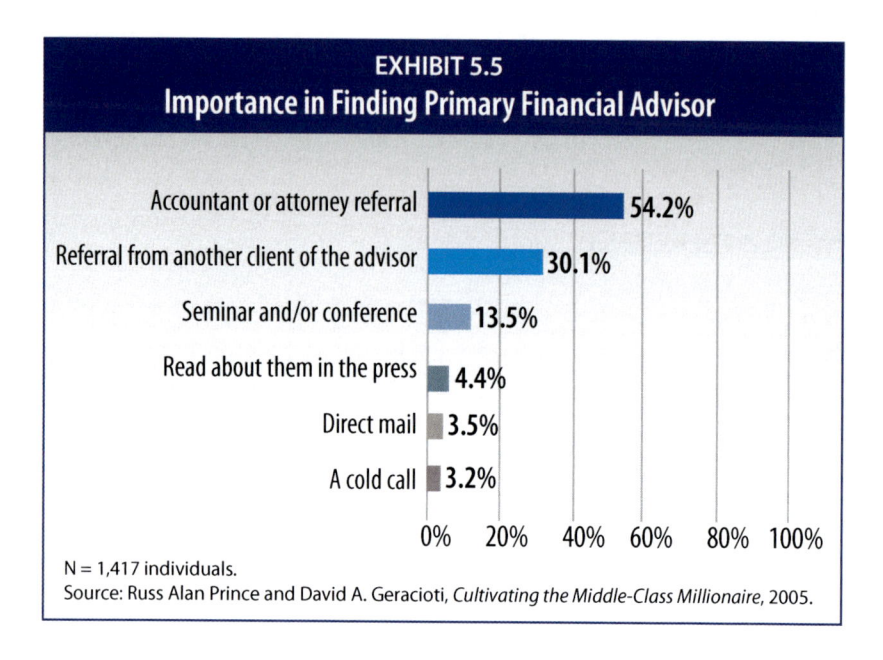

Source	Percentage
Accountant or attorney referral	54.2%
Referral from another client of the advisor	30.1%
Seminar and/or conference	13.5%
Read about them in the press	4.4%
Direct mail	3.5%
A cold call	3.2%

N = 1,417 individuals.
Source: Russ Alan Prince and David A. Geracioti, *Cultivating the Middle-Class Millionaire*, 2005.

interest in each partner to help the other grow. This agreement creates the "economic glue" that holds together a mutually beneficial partnership. The agreement is a formalized ongoing relationship that has been clearly spelled out and committed to by both sides and sets the stage for a long-term profitable relationship for both parties. At the heart of the agreement is a set of genuine benefits to the other professional, which results in additional revenue to the other firm.

Strategic alliances work, ultimately, because they enable you and your strategic partner to serve your clients better. Through the alliance, clients will benefit from both the expertise of the trusted professional with whom they already have a relationship and from your skills as a wealth manager who can address the full range of their financial concerns. And they can be assured that these professionals are working together as a team to maximize the probability that their clients achieve their financial goals.

The Opportunity for Strategic Alliances with CPAs

Again and again, our research has found that when CPA firms rely on strategic alliances with financial advisors to deliver some or all of their financial services to their clients, they realize substantially higher net incomes from financial services than do CPA firms that deliver these services directly. As you begin to approach potential CPA strategic partners, this perspective will give you confidence that what you are proposing will be extremely valuable to those professionals.

A brief look at just some of the data from the most recent study, *Succeeding Amid Adversity*, will give you an idea of the importance of strategic alliances to CPAs. In this study, we carried out a comprehensive survey of CPA firms around the country that are offering financial services and products.

We found that about one-third of surveyed firms (33.7 percent) use an internal model to deliver financial services to clients. That is, they provide all their financial services and products through one or more employees or partners at the firm.

In contrast, a sizable majority of the firms (65.4 percent) use a collaborative model, whereby they provide financial services and products through employees or partners and through strategic arrangements with financial services providers outside the firm. These strategic arrangements included turnkey asset management programs (TAMPs), providing clients with referrals to select financial services professionals to access financial services and products, and formal strategic alliances or joint ventures with one or more financial professionals. So two of the three primary methods used by the collaborative firms for providing financial services rely on financial advisors outside the firm.

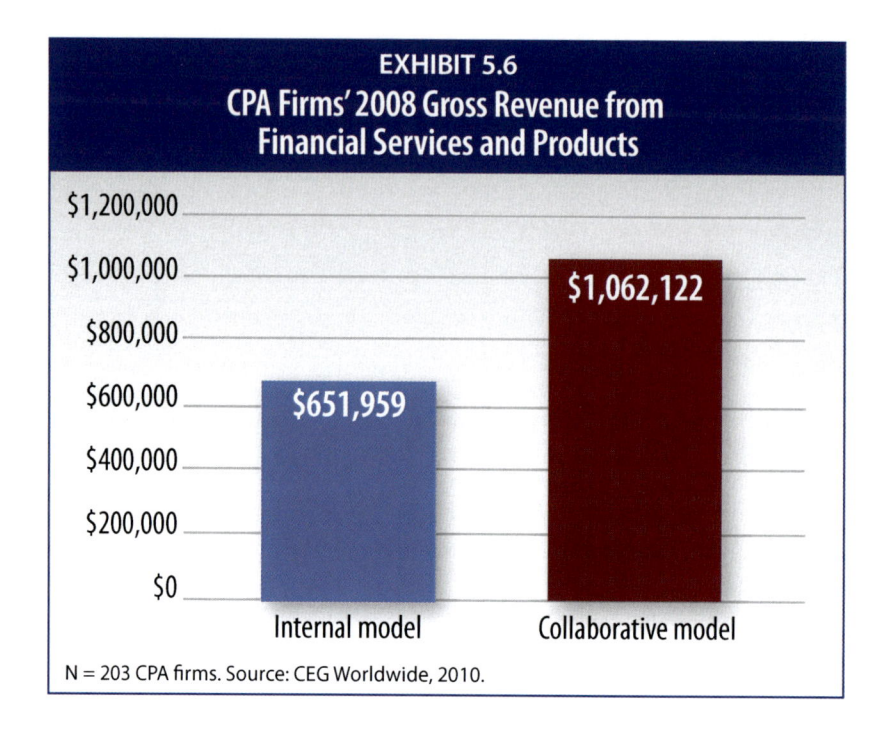

EXHIBIT 5.6
CPA Firms' 2008 Gross Revenue from Financial Services and Products

Model	Revenue
Internal model	$651,959
Collaborative model	$1,062,122

N = 203 CPA firms. Source: CEG Worldwide, 2010.

As **Exhibit 5.6** illustrates, the average revenue from financial services in 2008 for the firms using the internal model was $651,959, while financial services revenue for firms using the collaborative model topped $1 million.

We can assume that because collaborative firms rely on outside professionals to deliver a portion of their financial services, their costs to provide these services is lower than are the costs for firms using the internal model. These lower costs would translate into higher profit margins on their gross revenues.

What accounts for the collaborative firms' higher earnings from financial services compared to the earnings of firms that provide all financial services in-house? Above all, we believe it is their underlying embrace of strategic, collaborative relationships with outside professionals to deliver an optimal client experience.

We believe that these firms' willingness to turn to outside professionals comes primarily in response to market factors, including the greater complexity of financial products and increased client challenges due to market volatility. However, regardless of the reason, it provides you with a significant opportunity to build profitable strategic alliances with CPAs.

> **Ingredients for a Successful Alliance with a CPA**
>
> **Economic glue.** Do not form a strategic alliance unless there is a revenue share that creates "economic glue." We have simply found that without this economic glue, parties drift quickly apart or, worse, the CPA firm will decide to offer financial services without you.
>
> **Help from compliance.** Remember to work with your compliance department to make sure any agreement is properly drafted. It is important to note that accountants will need to be licensed.
>
> **No shortcuts.** Don't be tempted to try to do workarounds such as renting space or paying for the CPA firm's review of an investment plan. Don't work with anyone who's willing to cut corners. You're in this for the long haul—do it right.

The Opportunity for Strategic Alliances with Attorneys

The opportunities to grow your business by building strategic alliances do not end with CPAs. Another type of professional advisor—private client lawyers—has deep relationships in place with clients. By forming strategic alliances with these attorneys, you will gain access to their clients at the times when they most need your assistance. Most significantly, you will position yourself to receive referrals for clients who have just received inheritances or are in the process of restructuring key aspects of their financial lives.

Strategic alliances with these attorneys are quite specific. You will provide the expertise the attorneys need to enhance and build their businesses. In exchange, the attorneys will provide you with qualified affluent client referrals.

A successful strategic alliance with an attorney has several very attractive features:

- **The attorney refers affluent clients to you on a regular basis.** You will receive a steady stream of prequalified affluent clients for whom you can add significant value.

- **You are the primary financial advisor to whom the attorney makes referrals.** You will be first in the mind of the attorney when it comes

EXHIBIT 5.7
Contrasting Strategic Alliances with Accountants and Attorneys

Attribute	Strategic Alliances with Accountants	Strategic Alliances with Attorneys
Economic glue	Typically takes the form of a revenue share.	Typically takes the form of indirect financial incentives, such as methods for enhancing the partner's business, in exchange for referrals.
Level of formality	Very formal.	Informal.
Point of contact	While initial contact is with a single partner, the alliance must gain the backing of all major firm partners.	Alliance is generally made one-on-one with a single member of the firm; other partners are not involved.
Type of accountant/attorney	Alliances may be with accountants in a range of specialties.	Alliances are primarily restricted to private client lawyers.

Source: CEG Worldwide.

to referrals. As a result, you will receive all or most of the attorney's **referrals**.

- **The attorney is actively looking to make referrals to you.** The attorney is motivated to make referrals to you and thus is always keeping an eye out for clients who are suitable for referral.

Strategic alliances with attorneys are in some respects similar to those with accountants. In other ways they are quite different, as shown in overview form in **Exhibit 5.7**.

As we mentioned, the type of attorney that offers the best prospects for a profitable strategic alliance is the private client lawyer. These attorneys already routinely make referrals for their wealthy clients to obtain the investment services they need. More often than not, those referrals result in business for the referred advisor. According to a study of 619 private client lawyers, an average of 10 percent of these attorneys are already referring their clients to investment professionals and the average amount of investable assets per client referred was $2.7 million. The study also found that nearly three-quarters (73.2 percent) of clients used the financial advisors referred by their attorneys.

The study also showed that many private client lawyers—24.7 percent of those surveyed—are actively looking for eligible clients to refer. Perhaps best of all, the referral potential for financial advisors appears to remain largely untapped. Three out of four of the lawyers surveyed had not been approached by a single investment professional in the previous year. This spells opportunity for those financial advisors who do take the initiative in contacting private client lawyers.

The Consultative Strategic Alliance Process

We believe that strategic alliances should be built with the same type of systematic, fine-tuned process that you use for building long-term relationships with your clients.

As with the consultative wealth management process, each meeting builds on the previous one to deepen the relationship with the strategic partner and his or her firm and to methodically uncover opportunities to serve your mutual clients well as you help one another to grow your businesses. (See **Exhibit 5.8** for an overview of the five meetings.)

EXHIBIT 5.8
The Five Meetings of the Consultative Strategic Alliance Process

Meeting	Actions
Exploratory Meeting	• Assess chemistry with potential partner. • Interview champion. • Determine probable potential. • Decide together whether to continue with process.
Brainstorming Meetings	• Interview other decision-makers. • Gain deeper knowledge of the firm. • Identify additional opportunities.
Strategic Action Plan Development Meeting	• Present proposed strategic action plan to champion. • Gather input and make refinements.
Strategic Action Plan Presentation Meeting	• Present plan to all decision-makers. • Gather input and make refinements.
Ongoing Meetings	• Check in on progress of planned action items. • Review overall relationship and identify further opportunities.

WATCH THE VIDEO ▶ **Strategic Alliances with Professionals**
With John Bowen
www.cegworldwide.com/btbook/strategic-alliances-with-professionals

There's no doubt that there are significant opportunities out there for advisors to form strategic alliances with CPAs and private client lawyers as well as with a range of other professional advisors. Ultimately, these alliances represent a triple win that benefits you, your strategic partner and, most important, your clients. If you are endeavoring to manage your practice as a business, the subject we'll turn to next, it certainly makes good sense to consider initiating such strategic relationships while you stay focused on capturing additional assets and gaining referrals from existing clients.

Chapter 6
Manage Your Practice as a Business

We are part of a great industry, one that most of us joined in order to be great financial advisors helping clients achieve their most important dreams. Part of being great financial advisors is recognizing that we must also be great entrepreneurs—entrepreneurs who happen to have chosen the financial services industry.

There's a huge difference here. Your decision to become a great financial advisor or to become a great entrepreneur who is also a financial advisor will determine not only how profitable you are, but how much impact you have on your clients.

To become a great entrepreneur, you must learn to say "no" and to embrace the reality that you can't work with everyone who comes along. Instead, as we discussed in Chapter 3, you must take on only those clients who are right for you. With these ideal clients in place, you can focus on creating systems and processes that enable you to profitably and consistently deliver an experience that absolutely thrills and delights your clients.

In essence, you will build world-class systems to provide highly customized services for your ideal clients—services that are right on the money and that reliably meet or exceed their expectations. We believe that it's not only possible but downright necessary for you to leverage your efforts in a systematic manner.

Consider the first meeting with a prospective client. Financial advisors who are primarily focused on being great advisors might spend a lot of time describing the intricacies of their "unique" investment solutions and how those solutions can maximize the probability of the client achieving his or her goals. But advisors who are determined to become great entrepreneurs will have highly refined processes in place—such as the carefully planned Discovery Meeting and Total Client Profile processes we described in Chapter 4—that are highly efficient and tightly focused on the client. In the long run, these processes will deliver a consistently superior client experience as they help ideal clients more effectively achieve their goals.

Similarly, while a financial advisor might be able to design advanced planning solutions in a one-off fashion, the entrepreneur is ensured of arriving at the optimal advanced planning solutions for each client through the well-managed professional network process that he or she has put in place.

Great entrepreneurship for financial advisors boils down to clarity of purpose (identifying and serving the right clients), focus (creating a compelling value proposition) and execution (systematically delivering the client experience promised by your value proposition). You also must have the support mechanisms that will enable you to do what you love— profitably helping clients achieve their financial goals—over and over again, in a way that does not consume your entire life. (Many advisors are in this business because they love helping others. Ironically, when these advisors fail to run their businesses well, they are the ones who often become overwhelmed.)

Your goal is to build a simple, elegant wealth management business that runs systematically and almost automatically grows in value over time. To create such a great business, you must have the absolute clarity and focused execution needed to achieve your vision. In short, you have to manage your practice as a business. In this chapter we will cover five critical ways of doing this:

- Create a compelling vision.
- Build an effective business plan.
- Use technology wisely.
- Blueprint your systems and processes.
- Deliver "WOW" service.

WATCH THE VIDEO ▶ **Profile in Success: Christine Armstrong**
Boston, Massachusetts
www.cegworldwide.com/btbook/christine-armstrong

Create a Compelling Vision

To be successful on purpose, you need to be 100 percent clear about what you are doing. Not only will this clarity boost your own performance, it will motivate and unify your staff, business partners, other stakeholders and even your clients. A clear vision is an emotional lighthouse that will continuously pull you and your team toward your objectives. As Stephen Covey eloquently put it, to maximize the likelihood of success, you must "begin with the end in mind."

By clearly defining your vision, you will know precisely where you want to take your business and be able to accurately judge whether you're heading in the right direction. Many studies have shown that when business leaders effectively communicate a compelling vision of the future, their constituents report significantly higher levels of these success factors:

- Job satisfaction
- Commitment and loyalty

- Esprit de corps
- Clarity about organizational values
- Organizational pride
- Organizational productivity
- Retention of clients and staff

Make sure your vision consists of bite-size pieces—manageable portions. You'll be able to more easily communicate these smaller pieces to your stakeholders, construct a business plan from them and be able to execute them to achieve early wins. When the going occasionally gets tough—as it does for everyone—the clarity of your vision will determine whether you and your staff are overwhelmed or remain enthusiastic and tenaciously effective. With a clear vision, you'll find yourself jumping out of bed each morning, raring to get going.

The following vision-creation process has proven very useful to advisors in our coaching programs:

Step 1. Create

Start by creating a compelling vision of success—an exciting picture of what your business will look like three years from now when you have successfully built a world-class wealth management practice. Take some time to ask yourself why you're in the business, what you are hoping to achieve and how you will make it happen. You are a unique individual, and your vision must uniquely represent who you are, what's important to you, and how through your own hard work and determination you'll make it all happen.

Step 2. Communicate

To have maximum impact, you must communicate your vision effectively to your business partners, clients and other constituents. To motivate people, communicate your vision in a clear, lively manner. Describe it in a simple and direct way that moves and touches people. The word "inspire" means "to breathe life into." Leaders breathe life into their visions by the skill with which they communicate them. Use metaphors; analogies; examples; anecdotes and powerful images; and a positive, expressive communication style to bring your vision to life for others.

Step 3. Act

Most important, you must act to make the future you envision a reality. As futurist Joel Barker said,

> *"Vision without action is merely a dream.*
> *Action without vision just passes the time.*
> *Vision with action can change the world."*

Build a Strategic Business Plan

Once you have created your compelling vision and have tested it out on a few people inside and outside of your office, begin to act by constructing a thoughtful business plan around it. Successful people are intentional and do things on purpose. Activity alone is not enough—value is derived only from deliberate action. A well-crafted business plan can ensure that your actions are intentional and focused on clear aims. Plan for success and you will dramatically increase the odds of realizing that success.

For most financial advisors a traditional, formal business plan is unnecessary. Instead, we recommend a streamlined one-page plan that will focus you and your team squarely on the key goals you want to achieve and the steps required to achieve them.

Exhibit 6.1 shows the business plan template that we coach financial advisors in our programs to use. (In fact, we use the same template at CEG Worldwide to define our goals and actions as we grow our business.) You may access a PDF of this template at www.cegworldwide.com/downloads/ bt-book/eb_ceg_strategic_biz_plan.pdf. We suggest that you download and print the file and then complete it according to the instructions below.

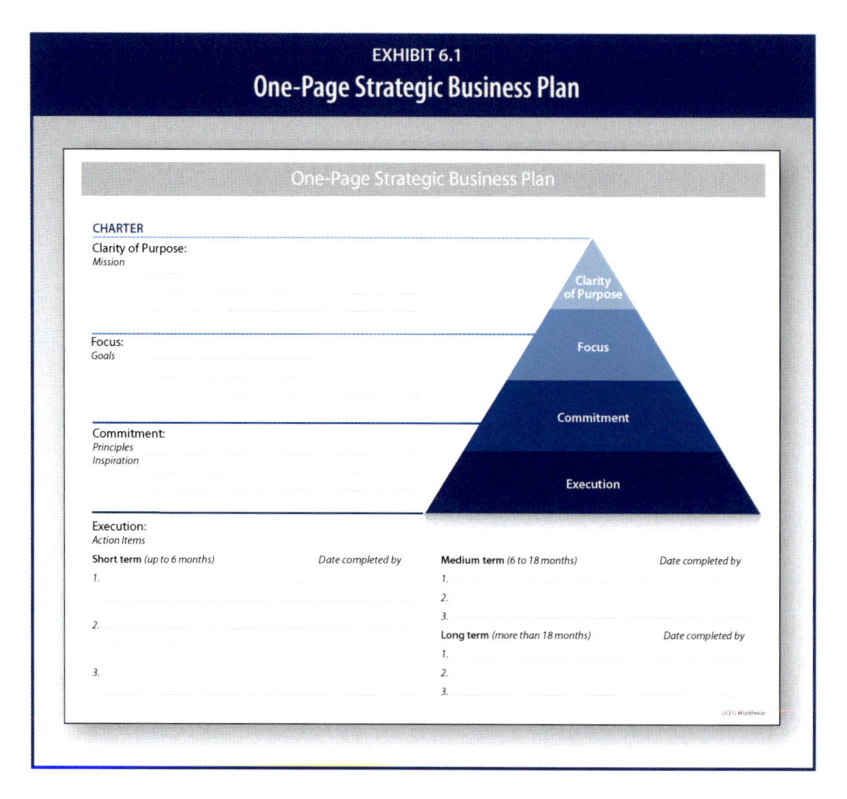

EXHIBIT 6.1
One-Page Strategic Business Plan

One-Page Strategic Business Plan

CHARTER
Clarity of Purpose:
Mission

Focus:
Goals

Commitment:
Principles
Inspiration

Execution:
Action Items

Short term *(up to 6 months)* — Date completed by
1.
2.
3.

Medium term *(6 to 18 months)* — Date completed by
1.
2.
3.

Long term *(more than 18 months)* — Date completed by
1.
2.
3.

Pyramid: Clarity of Purpose / Focus / Commitment / Execution

The pyramid in the upper-left corner sets out the four major parts of your plan:

- **Clarity of purpose:** What do you want to do? What is the primary mission of your business? More than likely, you defined this when you created your compelling vision. Write it down in just one or two sentences in the box at the upper right.

- **Focus:** These are your goals. What exactly do you want to achieve? Be specific; your goals could include items such as the types of clients

[120]

you want to work with or the income you want to earn. Describe these succinctly in the second box on the right.

- **Commitment:** You will not achieve your goals alone. Your partners and/or team must be with you in the greater purposes you are pursuing. In the third box at right, briefly describe what a fully committed team will look like.

- **Execution:** List the specific actions you will take in the short term (up to six months), medium term (six to 18 months) and long term (more than 18 months.) Do not overcommit—define no more than three action items for each time period. As you define your goals, make sure each item is SMART: Specific, Measurable, Achievable, Results-oriented and Time-bound.

Take a few minutes to update the action items on a regular basis as you accomplish tasks and define new ones. Place your strategic plan in a prominent place in your office so that you and your team members see it daily.

WATCH THE VIDEO ▶ **Run Your Practice Like a Business**
With John Bowen
www.cegworldwide.com/btbook/run-practice-like-business

Use Technology Wisely

When it comes to technology, we live in the best of times and the worst of times. On the one hand, technology today is more useful and—dare we say it—cooler than ever before. Even more than that, the pace at which new and useful technology is introduced is constantly accelerating.

On the other hand, no matter how cool or useful your technology is, it will help you grow your business only when it frees you up to do what's really important.

Both research and our experience consistently show that the most successful advisors spend the lion's share of their time on two key activities:

- Client relationship management

- Business development

This bears repeating: Technology is valuable only when it enables you to spend time on these key activities. If you don't use technology wisely, you'll waste enormous amounts of time on activities that seem relevant and useful (answering emails, playing phone tag, surfing the Web) but actually amount to significant time drains.

The best advisors keep abreast of new technological developments but only adopt or upgrade technology when it supports their relationship management or business development tasks. Here are the four areas of technology that you should keep on top of:

1. **Client-related tools.** These are tools that your clients and prospective clients come directly into contact with, including email, your Web site, an email newsletter, any webinars you may conduct and any social media tools you may use.

2. **Productivity-related tools.** These technologies are designed to enhance your efficiency and productivity. Under this category comes an efficient phone system; a good client relationship management software program (a must-have, because nothing is more valuable than your client relationships); a digital voice recorder; other standard office productivity programs and utilities for word processing, graphics generation, document backup and storage, voice recognition, document management and collaboration, Web conferencing, and presentation and training; virtual assistants; and mobile devices such as tablets and smartphones.

3. **Technical support tools.** These provide all your financial services solutions and include client profiling and research tools, your back-office platform (typically through your broker-dealer or custodian),

portfolio management and reporting software, financial planning software, online compliance support (if you don't have access to a compliance officer), and stock-option planning software.

4. **Time management tools.** These are processes and technologies that help you get the most from your limited time. You must deal efficiently with emails, voice mails and phone calls, which otherwise can be hugely distracting. It's also important to run effective—and, whenever possible, brief—meetings and to set an overall open-door management style that still lets you have your door closed most of the time. Random interruptions and socializing will kill your overall productivity.

With so many technologies available, you must choose your tools carefully and then use them effectively—without getting in over your head. Here are four simple rules for maximizing your use of technology:

1. **Stay slightly behind the leading edge.** Keep current, but stay away from the "bleeding edge"—you don't need to be a first adopter of any new technology.

2. **Don't develop new technology on your own (even if you can) or pay someone to develop new technology for you.** There's almost always an off-the-shelf solution that will do whatever you need to have done.

3. **Regularly assess your use of technology.** Ask yourself whether the technology you use actually enhances your productivity and frees you up for your core competencies and activities. Pay attention to what other top advisors you know are doing so that you don't fall too far behind in any key area.

4. **Rely on the advice of true experts.** To keep your time free for your most important activities, turn to trusted technology providers for help. For example, if your telephone and voice-mail system is out of

date, don't spend time researching options. Find a professional who can rapidly present you with solid recommendations and then take the work all the way through to conclusion. Also, when implementing new software programs, take advantage of training programs offered by the vendor. Experts estimate that we use only 20 percent of the capabilities of most software programs. Make sure your staff members are true experts and that you are getting maximum return on your investment through in-depth training on key software programs.

Careful technology choices will certainly support your relationship management and business development efforts, but don't for one minute think that technology will create a profitable-on-purpose business where there wasn't one before. Technology is a tool—use it wisely or it will end up using you.

Blueprint Systems and Processes

Successful entrepreneurs excel at creating compelling visions for their businesses. Working from their visions, they build the systems and processes they need and that will create a meaningful competitive advantage by differentiating themselves from their competitors in their customers' eyes.

Often, however, these systems and processes exist only in the mind of the entrepreneur or a key staff person and are not documented. This causes two problems. First, the systems never become a clear reality for anyone else in the firm. Second, because the systems exist only in someone's mind, they are impossible to maintain in the absence of that person.

By establishing repeatable systems and processes, you create a defined experience—both externally (for clients and prospective clients) and internally (for team members)—for everyone who comes into contact with the business. And when you document, or blueprint, those processes, the documentation itself increases the strategic value of your business. You will have a turnkey operation that almost anyone could run, even if you are no longer part of the firm.

In short, you need to create and blueprint both systems and processes that deliver great results without relying on extraordinary personal intervention by you or your staff. This is the only way to ensure consistent, outstanding experiences for both your affluent clients and your team members, whether you are there or not. And it's the only way to assure potential strategic buyers, either now or in the future, that the success of your practice is not solely dependent on your presence.

There are two major categories of systems and processes that you should build, master and blueprint for your business. The first consists of your **client experience systems**, which act outside of the firm and are dedicated to acquiring, servicing and communicating with affluent clients. The second major category is made up of your **business systems**. These internal systems are responsible for efficient management, profit generation and equity creation.

Every system and process should be precisely defined, perfected and blueprinted. Don't try to do all this blueprinting by yourself to the detriment of your most important activities—managing client relationships and business development. Instead, assign one or more key team members to undertake the blueprinting process in a reasonable time frame with your guidance and assistance.

When the blueprinting is complete, make sure that everyone in your organization has access to all the blueprints. Invite them to comment on and improve them. Your team members—who actually carry out the majority of the blueprinted systems and processes on a daily basis—will often have the best ideas about how to make things run even better.

Deliver WOW Service

"WOW!" That's what you want to hear your clients say to you and, more important, about you. At its heart, WOW service entails raising the bar to deliver each client a world-class experience—one that differentiates you

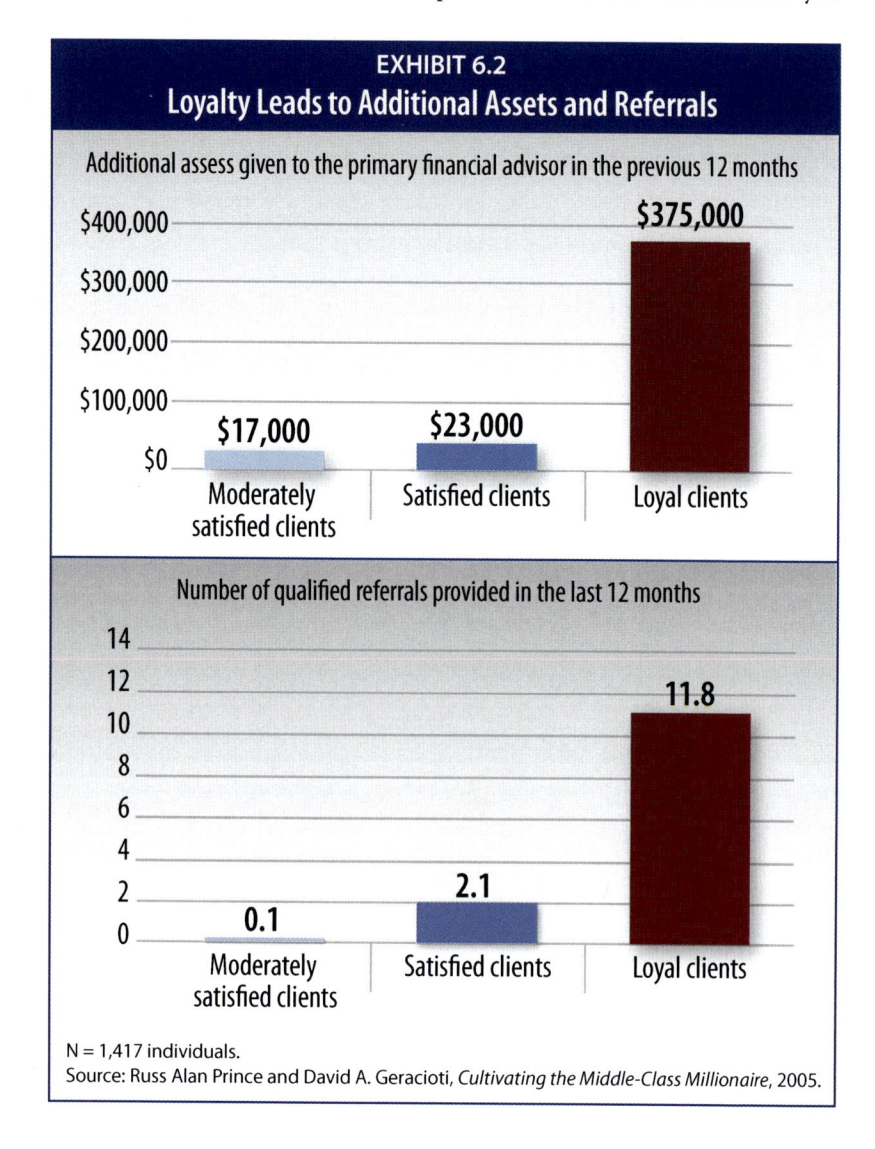

EXHIBIT 6.2
Loyalty Leads to Additional Assets and Referrals

Additional assess given to the primary financial advisor in the previous 12 months

Client Type	Additional Assets
Moderately satisfied clients	$17,000
Satisfied clients	$23,000
Loyal clients	$375,000

Number of qualified referrals provided in the last 12 months

Client Type	Referrals
Moderately satisfied clients	0.1
Satisfied clients	2.1
Loyal clients	11.8

N = 1,417 individuals.
Source: Russ Alan Prince and David A. Geracioti, *Cultivating the Middle-Class Millionaire*, 2005.

and your firm in a way that clients find unforgettable and competitors find difficult to match. By creating processes that ensure a consistent high-quality experience at every point of contact, you will evoke pure delight in your clients. And not just delight, but the motivation to provide you with more business. As **Exhibit 6.2** shows, the most satisfied, loyal clients give their advisors significantly more assets to manage and make many more qualified referrals than do less-satisfied

What It Means to WOW

WOW is synonymous with *delight, dazzle* and *astound*. To build a world-class business, you must go much further than merely satisfying your clients. You can't just talk the customer satisfaction talk—you and everyone on your team who comes into contact with clients must live and breathe client satisfaction.

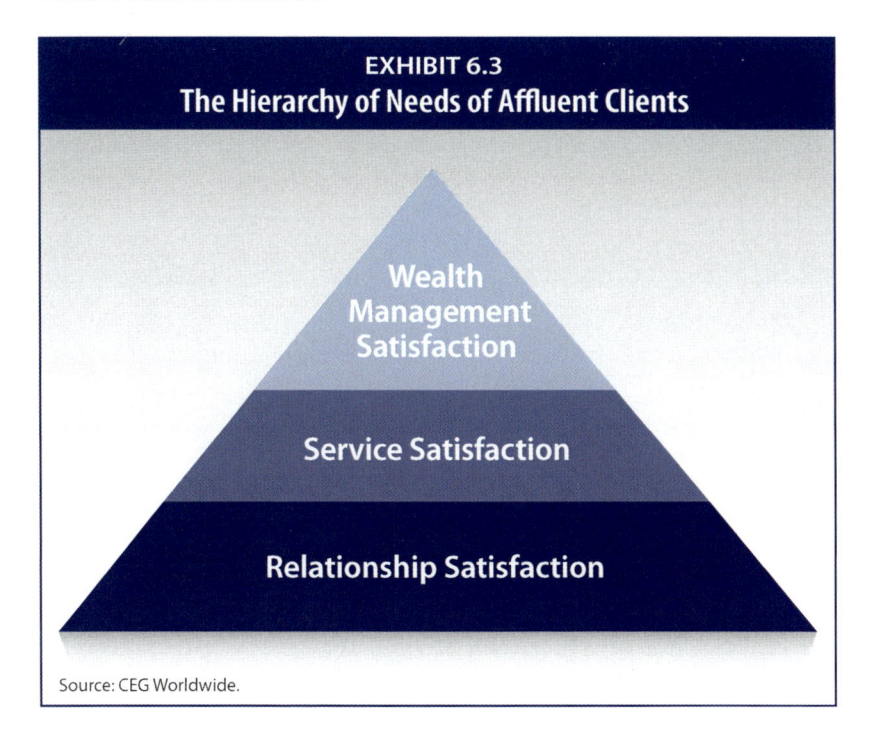

EXHIBIT 6.3
The Hierarchy of Needs of Affluent Clients

- Wealth Management Satisfaction
- Service Satisfaction
- Relationship Satisfaction

Source: CEG Worldwide.

What would it mean for your firm to deliver WOW service? To answer this question, consider exactly what clients really need. **Exhibit 6.3** shows a three-step pyramid of affluent clients' hierarchy of needs.

Relationship satisfaction forms the base of the pyramid, and requires strong, ongoing personal interactions and connections between you and your affluent clients. Except in those rare cases when a client expresses a preference for minimal contact, it is essential to communicate more frequently with your clients—especially about something other than their investment accounts and performance.

Our 2011 survey found that that top-earning financial advisors understand and act on the importance of client contact to build relationships. As you can see from **Exhibit 6.4**, the financial advisors earning more than $1 million a year contacted each of their top 20 clients an average of 28.0 times over the previous year—far more than financial advisors in all other income groups.

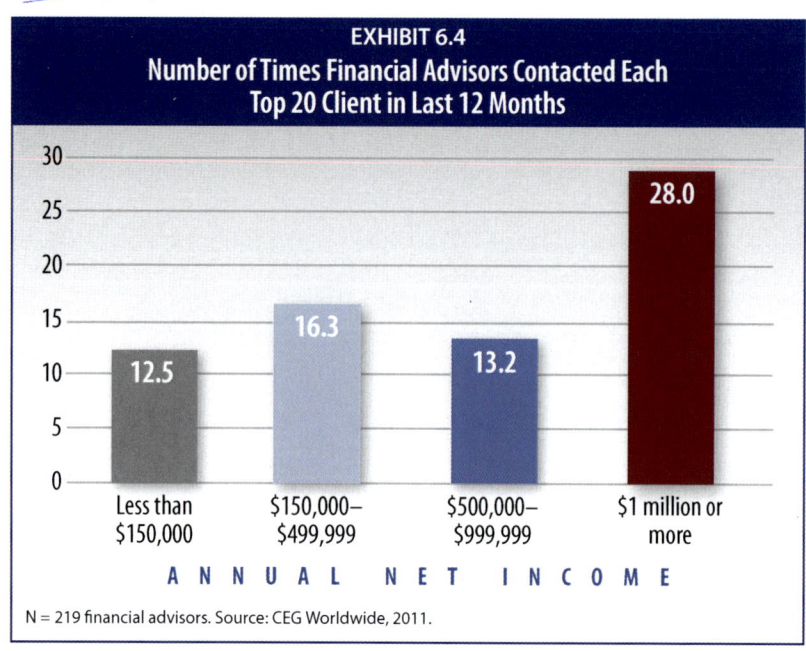

EXHIBIT 6.4
Number of Times Financial Advisors Contacted Each Top 20 Client in Last 12 Months

Annual Net Income	Times Contacted
Less than $150,000	12.5
$150,000–$499,999	16.3
$500,000–$999,999	13.2
$1 million or more	28.0

N = 219 financial advisors. Source: CEG Worldwide, 2011.

Our previous industry studies have repeatedly found direct links between the amount of client contact and client satisfaction, client loyalty and willingness to provide introductions to qualified prospective clients. This study clearly shows that this common theme of financial advisor success continues to endure.

Second on the pyramid, and built on top of relationship satisfaction, is **service satisfaction**. Affluent clients expect a high level of administrative and account service. If you frequently fail at these, your wealthy clients will most likely look for a new advisor. Given that problems will inevitably occur—however infrequently—you need constructive processes in place to quickly resolve these service failures.

Wealth management satisfaction sits at the top of the pyramid, supported by strong relationship and service satisfaction. The reason clients come to you in the first place is for assistance in addressing their financial challenges and achieving their financial goals. An effective, comprehensive wealth management process is essential to address your clients' varied and often complex financial issues.

Relationship satisfaction forms the base of the pyramid for good reason. Clients who are unhappy with short-term investment performance are far more likely to remain with you if they experience high relationship satisfaction. Likewise, a strong advisor-client relationship will help smooth out the inevitable bumps with respect to both service satisfaction and wealth management satisfaction.

Therefore, we turn next to how to manage your client relationships to ensure relationship satisfaction.

WATCH THE VIDEO ▶ **The Right Amount of Client Contact**
With John Bowen
www.cegworldwide.com/btbook/right-amount-of-client-contact

The Seven Client Satisfaction Factors

Human relationships are complex, and no two client relationships are alike. Research has identified seven factors that are consistently aligned with a high level of client satisfaction. (See **Exhibit 6.5**.) To assess these factors, contrast the feelings of very satisfied clients with those of the very dissatisfied clients. Doing so will highlight the key elements of client satisfaction.

1. The Competence Factor

Managing the wealth of the affluent automatically assumes a reasonable level of financial and investment competence. For this reason, even clients who were very dissatisfied with their advisors were still likely to rate them high in the area of competence. For example, 80.6 percent of very dissatisfied clients gave their advisors credit for money management expertise—nearly the same as the 80.9 percent of very satisfied clients who did so. Very dissatisfied clients rated their advisors somewhat lower in the areas of confidentiality and knowledge about investments but still gave relatively high marks.

Since clients already assume competence, it's not a huge factor in determining client satisfaction. At the same time, this doesn't mean that you shouldn't justify your clients' view of your competence. Most of the items that you create through your credibility marketing efforts—including articles, white papers and books—will serve to reinforce your affluent clients' belief in your competence as a wealth manager.

2. The Hustle Factor

While competence is largely taken for granted, the same is not true of hustle—going the extra mile. This is seen most sharply in clients' views of their advisors' perfectionism. Fully 61.7 percent of very satisfied clients

EXHIBIT 6.5
Seven Key Factors That Affect Client Satisfaction

	Very Satisfied Clients	Very Dissatisfied Clients
The Competence Factor		
Keeping dealings confidential	82.6%	64.5%
Having money management expertise	80.9%	80.6%
Being knowledgeable in investments	72.3%	64.5%
The Hustle Factor		
Being extremely reliable	81.7%	54.8%
Being a perfectionist	61.7%	6.5%
The No-Surprises Factor		
Wanting to know complaints	55.3%	6.5%
Communicating about problems and solutions	38.3%	0.0%
The Warmth Factor		
Being responsive	74.9%	45.2%
Being warm	64.3%	25.8%
The First-to-Know Factor		
Providing timely information	77.9%	19.4%
Giving regular client briefings	75.3%%	38.7%
The Listening Factor		
Being patient while explaining	82.6%	54.8%
Listening well	78.7%	48.4%
The Client-Centered Factor		
Understandng specific needs	75.7%	25.8%
Providing viable alternatives	75.3%	41.9%
Defining client needs	59.1%	12.9%

N = 879 affluent clients.
Source: Russ Alan Prince and Karen Maru File, *Cultivating the Affluent.*

saw their advisors as being perfectionists, compared with only 6.5 percent of very dissatisfied clients.

The key to high marks in hustle? Reliability. When you make a promise, keep it and keep it on time. Set a goal of providing perfect service, with plenty of attention to details.

3. The No-Surprises Factor

While clients dislike service failures, they dislike unpleasant surprises even more, making it your job to prevent them as much as possible. While more than half (55.3 percent) of very satisfied clients felt that their advisors wanted to hear their complaints and feedback, a mere 6.5 percent of very dissatisfied clients felt this way. Likewise, not a single very dissatisfied client believed that his or her advisor looked at failures as opportunities to provide better service by communicating about the problem and possible solutions, while 38.3 percent of very satisfied clients did.

To rate well with your clients in this area, you should actively solicit candid feedback, including negative perceptions, from your clients. Not only will this help you spot and head off major problems, it will clearly demonstrate your concern about service to your clients. In addition, whenever an external disaster occurs (such as the September 11, 2001, attacks), immediately get in touch—and stay in touch—with your clients.

4. The Warmth Factor

Responsiveness and sincere warmth are another important part of client satisfaction. Three-quarters (74.9 percent) of very satisfied clients saw their advisors as very responsive, compared with less than half (45.2 percent) of very dissatisfied clients. When asked if their advisors are warm, 64.3 percent of highly satisfied clients said yes, while only one-quarter of dissatisfied clients had this response.

It's important to understand that good manners and being polite are not enough—virtually all clients, satisfied and dissatisfied, believe that their advisors are generally courteous. Affluent clients are looking for more: true emotional warmth. Keep this in mind as you make your hiring decisions. If your staff (or you) needs help in this area, there are workshops that can help improve interpersonal skills, as will practice.

5. The First-to-Know Factor

Your clients want to be kept informed not just about their portfolios and financial progress, but also about important changes at your firm and with your staff. Don't let your clients hear about personnel changes when they are in need and call your office or from a competing advisor—this is exactly the type of negative surprise you want to avoid.

Very satisfied clients score their advisors well in this area, with 77.9 percent reporting that their advisors provided information in a timely manner, and 75.3 percent acknowledging their advisors' efforts to give regular briefings. As can be expected, very dissatisfied clients scored their advisors poorly here, with just 19.4 percent feeling that they received timely information from their advisors.

Given how important it is to affluent clients to be the "first to know," it would be wise to incorporate tools into your client database that allow you to red-flag situations and issues that call for you to be in touch with clients.

6. The Listening Factor

As you well know by now, affluent clients want advisors who pay attention to them. Listening skills are therefore another important element in the client satisfaction equation. Of very satisfied clients, 82.6 percent thought that their advisors were willing to be patient and take as much time as needed to explain things, compared with 54.8 percent of dissatisfied clients. Likewise, a significantly greater number of satisfied clients believed their advisors spent enough time listening.

Too often advisors believe they must educate their clients, as opposed to listening to them as they speak of their needs, fears and wants. Your goal, as always, should be to learn more about your affluent clients through attentive listening.

7. The Client-Centered Factor

Affluent clients generally care little about your other clients. What they do care about is having you focus on them and their individual needs. Your ability to convey the sense to each client that you are striving to both understand his or her unique needs and then provide individualized solutions is absolutely critical.

Specifically, 75.7 percent of the satisfied clients felt that their advisors made a significant effort to understand their unique needs, as compared with only 25.8 percent of dissatisfied clients. Also revealing on this point: Three-quarters (75.3 percent) of the very satisfied thought they received well-thought-out solutions suited to their needs, contrasted with 41.9 percent of the dissatisfied.

WATCH THE VIDEO ▶ **Great Client Communication**
With John Bowen
www.cegworldwide.com/btbook/great-client-communication

The WOW Service Checklist

The following is a checklist of the factors that matter most to affluent clients and that lead to the highest levels of client satisfaction. The factors are grouped according to the three levels of the hierarchy of needs of affluent clients, starting at the bottom of the pyramid with relationship satisfaction, next moving up to service satisfaction and then to wealth management satisfaction. For your convenience, you may download a PDF of the checklist at www.cegworldwide.com/downloads/bt-book/eb_ceg_wow_checklist.pdf.

The WOW Service Checklist

1. Relationship Satisfaction

- ❑ The financial advisor is emotionally warm and sympathetic and reassuring as needed.
- ❑ The advisor is honest and open at all times.
- ❑ The advisor is good at remembering personal details about clients.
- ❑ The advisor always keeps clients' interests at heart.
- ❑ The advisor always encourages clients to bring up any issue or question of importance.
- ❑ The advisor takes as much time as necessary to explain issues to clients yet never wastes clients' time.
- ❑ The advisor never shows impatience.
- ❑ The advisor spends an unusual amount of time listening closely to clients' needs, fears, wants and desires.
- ❑ The advisor does unexpected and thoughtful things for clients.
- ❑ The advisor and all team members make each client feel extremely important.
- ❑ The advisor ascertains the type and frequency of contact each client wants and then provides exactly that contact.
- ❑ The advisor incorporates high-net-worth psychology into every contact.
- ❑ The advisor diplomatically handles communication mistakes made by clients.
- ❑ The advisor provides clients with ample information in writing as appropriate.
- ❑ The advisor provides each client with a detailed agenda for every meeting.
- ❑ The advisor introduces clients to qualified experts and other important individuals.
- ❑ The advisor provides regular updates about the practice's programs and operations.
- ❑ The advisor encourages clients to read the practice's promotional materials.
- ❑ The advisor actively encourages clients to suggest ways of improving operations and services.
- ❑ The advisor encourages clients to ask friends, family and associates about how they perceive the firm and its services.

2. Service Satisfaction

- ❑ The advisor always delivers within the promised time frame on the commitments he or she makes.
- ❑ Client accounts do not suffer from administrative errors.
- ❑ The advisor keeps all client information and dealings completely confidential.
- ❑ The advisor is always a perfectionist.
- ❑ The advisor involves each client in decision-making to the extent the client prefers.
- ❑ Services are truly customized to fit the needs of each client.
- ❑ The advisor always provides timely information to every client.
- ❑ The advisor immediately gets in touch with clients when a major external event or disaster occurs.
- ❑ The advisor has a methodology in place to red-flag situations that require client contact.
- ❑ The quality of service consistently exceeds client expectations.
- ❑ The advisor or team member responds within the promised time frame to all client requests or telephone calls.
- ❑ The firm offers a dedicated toll-free phone line for clients.
- ❑ The firm offers a comprehensive user-friendly Web site that provides clients access to their portfolio information.
- ❑ The advisor gives quick and complete responses to all questions.
- ❑ The team's key professionals are highly accessible to clients.
- ❑ Team members have appropriate access to client information to enable them to provide world-class service.
- ❑ The advisor frequently invites clients to provide feedback about the firm's or team's performance.
- ❑ The firm resolves all service failures in a timely fashion—when possible, on the same day they occur.
- ❑ The advisor views service failures as opportunities to provide great service by communicating about the problem and possible solutions.
- ❑ The advisor interviews all lost clients to determine and address their reasons for leaving.
- ❑ The firm occasionally uses an outside "mystery shopper" to assess levels of service and responsiveness.
- ❑ The firm periodically summarizes feedback on its own service performance and identifies areas for improvement.

3. Wealth Management Satisfaction

- ❑ The advisor makes an exceptional effort to understand each client's unique needs.
- ❑ The advisor works with all clients to define their needs in considerable detail.
- ❑ The advisor provides well-thought-out and viable alternatives suited to clients' specific needs, objectives and tolerance for risk.
- ❑ The advisor is knowledgeable about investments.
- ❑ Investment performance is consistent with clients' stated goals and objectives.
- ❑ Investment performance is good compared to indexes.
- ❑ Portfolio performance meets client expectations.

© Copyright 2013 CEG Worldwide, LLC.

You can use the checklist both to evaluate your own current service level and as something to aim for in the future.

Assessing Client Satisfaction

To establish and then fine-tune your delivery of WOW service, you need help from your clients. It would be easy to assume that you already know how clients perceive your firm, but if you really want to know, you must proactively invite feedback.

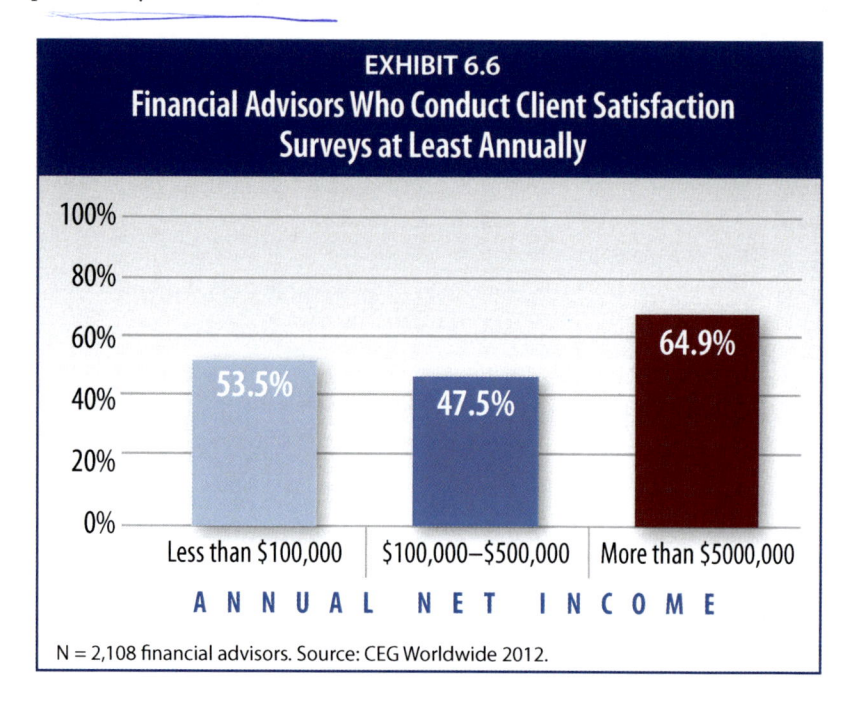

EXHIBIT 6.6
Financial Advisors Who Conduct Client Satisfaction Surveys at Least Annually

Annual Net Income	Percentage
Less than $100,000	53.5%
$100,000–$500,000	47.5%
More than $5000,000	64.9%

N = 2,108 financial advisors. Source: CEG Worldwide 2012.

To systematically collect this feedback, we recommend that you conduct a formal client survey every year. Such a survey gives your clients permission to point out where you could improve. It also sends a clear message that you care about them and their opinions, which will make them more willing to open up and help you explore how you can better serve them. Our research shows that many financial advisors are now doing this—as seen in **Exhibit 6.6**—but the highest-earning advisors are doing it most often.

If you are among the financial advisors who do not conduct regular surveys of your clients, we suggest that you start now. Build your questionnaire by choosing four or five items from each of the three major categories of the WOW service that you believe are most important to your clients' satisfaction. Ask clients to rate their level of agreement with each statement on a simple scale of 1 to 5.

Here is an example, using the first item from each of the three categories of the WOW service checklist:

On a scale of 1 to 5, with 1 being strongly disagree and 5 being strongly agree, please rate the following statements about your experience as a client with us:

- ___ Your financial advisor is emotionally warm and sympathetic and reassuring as needed.

- ___ Your financial advisor always delivers within the promised time frame on the commitments he or she makes.

- ___ Your financial advisor makes an exceptional effort to understand your unique needs.

Depending on your clients' preferences, you can administer your survey via one of the free online survey tools available or through the mail, providing a return envelope. Regardless of the method you choose, encourage frank answers by providing clients the option to respond anonymously.

After you have gathered, organized and distilled the survey information, share the results with your team members. Get their reactions and input on improving systems in response to the survey results. While you won't always get positive responses from your surveys, every response can be used to your advantage in some way. Your whole business can become more responsive to your clients from the ground up.

Once you have created a list of action items in response to the survey results, communicate these to your clients. Let them know specifically how you will be doing things differently as a result of their input.

With a clear understanding in place of how to manage your practice as a business, we turn next to how to manage and best work with other businesses, from financial institutions and wholesalers to providers of technology and other noncore functions.

Chapter 7
Partner with Institutions and Other Professionals

As an entrepreneurial advisor, you can't create a great business all on your own—nor should you try. As we have stressed throughout this book, you and your clients will be far better off if you focus on your core competencies and outsource everything else. If you are like most successful advisors, this means outsourcing everything but client relationship management, expert relationship management and business development.

Such outsourcing makes sense for three very good reasons. First, industry research consistently shows that advisors who spend more time on these core competencies do better financially. Second, in today's complex world, providing your clients with a great experience and across-the-board WOW service requires a depth of expertise that is simply beyond any one individual or team. This means that your clients will directly benefit from intelligent outsourcing. And third, by being smart about which institutions, wholesalers, and other outside professionals and services you work with, you'll gain valuable practice management tips and uncover additional opportunities. In short, effective outsourcing enables you to focus on what really matters.

Unfortunately, many financial advisors do not consciously choose their outsourcing partners. Instead, they end up working with particular institutions and other providers by accident and then become so busy with the day-to-day activities of their practices that they fail to take the time to consider what ideal partners would really look like.

As our industry has dramatically grown over the last decades, a wide variety of outside providers have made themselves readily available to assist financial advisors. Given the many potential providers who are competing for your business, if you're spending substantial time outside the scope of your core competencies, then you should make sure that you have a very compelling business reason for doing so. In this chapter, we will look at the two primary categories of outsourcing partners: financial institutions (and the wholesalers that work with them) and independent contractors.

Working with Financial Institutions and Their Wholesalers

All financial advisors—from wirehouse stockbrokers to independent broker-dealer representatives to registered investment advisors—work with financial institutions to one degree or another. At a minimum, you need custodial services from your brokerage firm or another custodian. To provide your clients with optimal solutions and WOW service, you need access to a variety of financial products and tools. As the idea of open architectures gains widespread acceptance, increasing numbers of advisors of all stripes are taking advantage of the benefits that come from working with multiple financial institutions. In our 2011 survey of financial advisors, one out of four (24.7 percent) reported being very or extremely concerned with obtaining needed resources from financial institutions.

As financial products become ever more commoditized, financial institutions recognize that they must rely on more than the quality of their products to differentiate themselves in the minds of advisors. To do so, they offer support and services designed to help advisors grow their businesses and serve their clients better and more profitably. Commonly called "value-based marketing," this support, usually offered through the financial institutions' wholesalers, is provided in three main areas:

1. **Sales and marketing:** helping advisors move upmarket by attracting affluent clients

2. **Practice management support:** disseminating the best practices of advisors to help them build more profitable businesses

3. **Technical support:** assistance with technical issues concerning the financial institution's products and services

Regardless of which financial institutions you are working with now—or are considering working with in the future—be thoughtful and choose your partners for the right reasons. Being able to accurately evaluate the offerings of institutions so that you can select the right ones will make a critical difference to the success of your business.

Identifying the Right Financial Institutions

To determine whether your current institutional partners are optimal for your practice, start with some self-analysis. We recommend using a consultative process similar to the one that we recommend you use with your clients to assist them in achieving their financial goals. Examine your practice and evaluate any existing or potential partners with the following four-step process.

Step 1. Be Introspective

Examine the quantitative part of your business. Identify your results over the last 12 months. Write down your net income, assets under management, assets that you influence and gross revenue. Also identify the number of client relationships, the number of qualified introductions you have received and the number of group presentations you have conducted during the last year.

Identify your current value proposition to your clients. What feedback do you receive from clients and prospective clients regarding your service offerings? Which additional elements will you need to significantly increase your business?

What would a new institutional partner bring to your business that your current partners are not offering? How would a new partner address the feedback you have received and provide the additional elements you need to meet the needs of your current and future clients?

Step 2. Develop a Clear Vision of Your Future

Is what you're doing today really what matters to you in the long run? Many of us get caught up in our ongoing activities and forget to focus on what's really important in our business and personal lives. What matters most gets buried under layers of pressing problems, immediate concerns and to-do lists. If you are serious about building a hugely successful business, you cannot afford to get lost in the mundane of the day-to-day.

Revisit the vision for your future that we recommended you develop. Do your current institutional partners fit into this picture? Do they actively support your vision? Or are they stumbling blocks to achieving it?

Step 3. Identify Goals Important to Realizing Your Vision

Make a list of the personal and business goals that are important to your vision and that you will commit to achieving over the next year. To be most effective, write down your commitments. Now ask yourself: Would changing any of my institutional partners increase the probability of achieving my goals?

Step 4. Evaluate Potential Partners

If your assessment reveals that your current partners are not optimal for building a world-class business, your next task is to identify partners who can fill that role for you. Accurately evaluating the offerings of financial institutions so that you can select the right ones will have a tremendous positive impact on your business. At the core of your decisions are two key questions:

1. Is the financial institution equipped to help me properly serve my market? You need to work with institutions that can support your move to a significantly higher level of success by enabling you to better serve your affluent clients.

2. If not, are the deficiencies severe enough to warrant moving to a new one? The time and money required to move to a new financial institution can be significant (this is particularly true of a switch to a new broker-dealer or clearing firm), so do not undertake a move without being sure that you can justify the costs.

These are not easy questions. To help you answer them, methodically assess the value proposition of your current financial institutions or of any institutions that you are considering partnering with. Your goal is to identify the institutions that will provide you and your clients the most net value, or the value gained minus the costs.

First assess the total value to you that an institution will provide, including these elements:

- Product value
- Service value
- Personnel value
- Image value

Then add up the total cost to you of working with that institution. Consider these costs:

- Monetary cost
- Time cost
- Energy cost
- Psychic cost

Finally, subtract the total costs from the total value that you receive, and you'll be in a much better position to make a final determination as to the institution in question. At that point, the choice is yours as to which institutions are right to serve as partners for you and your clients. Remember we are all judged by the company we keep.

Identifying the Right Wholesalers

Once you have chosen the best institutional partners to support your success, you can expect the wholesalers (often called "business development managers" or "business consultants") who represent these institutions to call on you. More often than not, you won't have a choice about the specific wholesalers you work with. Instead your choice will be whether you work with an assigned wholesaler or directly with the institution's internal wholesaler group.

As the go-between who connects companies offering financial products and services and the advisors who ultimately recommend those products and services to clients, wholesalers are an inevitable part of life in our business. Many financial advisors regard wholesalers as either a nuisance or a source of ongoing freebies. The overall advisor experience with wholesalers has been, at best, mixed. CEG Worldwide research conducted in 2007 found that working with a top-flight wholesaler was a concern for just half of 2,094 studied advisors. Of those working with mutual fund wholesalers, just 28.0 percent rated these wholesalers as "very good" or "excellent."

Despite this mixed experience, wholesalers can be invaluable resources and potent business-building partners—provided that you screen for the best ones and then work with them to maximum advantage. If you are proactive about identifying and working with the "A" players who have the ability to provide you with substantial value, you'll have serious business development partners who can help you build a truly great practice.

How, then, can you differentiate between wholesalers? To begin with, consider the differences between the three prominent wholesaler strategies:

1. **The educational strategy** includes value-based marketing programs, chiefly characterized by technical, prospecting, sales, practice management and other programs that are delivered through the wholesaler system.

2. **The field support strategy** focuses on your sales and marketing processes. Wholesalers can work with one of your clients directly or, at the other end of the continuum, develop comprehensive, targeted marketing materials for you to use with your clients.

3. **The consultative strategy** takes a much more intensive approach. Often wholesalers become business and practice management consultants to you, providing you with counsel on key aspects of your business by using the full resources of their financial institutions.

While these three value-based marketing strategies are not mutually exclusive, many financial institutions have decided to primarily focus on just one. Once you are clear about which type of strategy will deliver the most value to you and your clients, you can focus on developing relationships with the wholesalers who mainly follow that strategy.

As a general rule, we recommend that you focus on working with wholesalers who embrace the consultative approach. You want ongoing relationships with a small number of wholesalers who serve as outside business partners by providing you with valuable insight into how other successful advisors are growing their businesses. As "how-to-grow-your-business coaches" who serve as conduits of best practices and leverage their financial institutions' resources, these wholesalers can help you substantially grow your business and better serve your clients.

However, the educational and field support strategies can yield substantial value in certain circumstances. For example, if you have a client with a large concentrated stock position and neither you nor anyone on your team is well-versed enough in all the options available to deal effectively, then a good wholesaler may be able to quickly provide you with access to an in-house expert. Ultimately, as the wholesaler market matures, we believe that all three strategies will more and more frequently be used together to develop strong, multifaceted support programs.

The bottom line: Regardless of which strategy they follow, there are extremely qualified wholesalers out there who can be of tremendous assistance to you—but you need to be intentional about identifying them and working with them effectively. To recognize the best wholesalers, once again, you should begin with the end in mind and remember to place a great premium on your time—it's the one thing that you can never get back. Since your core competencies do not include responding to copious wholesaler phone calls or selecting the best possible wholesalers to work with, your first step is to train an assistant or someone in your office to undertake these activities.

When wholesalers call you—and they will—the screener should say something like this: "Mr. Smith works with a limited number of top wholesalers, so it's very important to him that wholesalers deliver a significant value in terms of helping him grow his business. I'd like to ask you a few questions to make sure your time with him would be well-spent." Such questions would include the following:

- "How do you typically work with financial advisors?"
- "Have you ever been a financial advisor? How does your previous experience help you meet the challenges that Mr. Smith faces?"
- "What kind of support do you typically provide to advisors?"
- "Can you give me some examples of best practices that you have shared with advisors who are working with [the advisor's specific target market]?"
- "Can you share some of the best sales ideas of the top advisors you work with that might be applicable to Mr. Smith's practice?"
- "Mr. Smith typically works on a consultative basis; rather than focusing on product sales, he works with each client through a systematic consulting process. How can you help him improve his consulting process while using your financial products?"
- "To what extent can you provide assistance in leading-edge, highly technical areas of wealth management to help Mr. Smith serve his clients better?"
- "Do you or does someone in your company provide additional practice management support that will help Mr. Smith run his business more efficiently and profitably?"
- "To what extent can you be Mr. Smith's personal coach to help him achieve all that he is capable of achieving?"

If it becomes clear that the wholesaler mainly follows the educational strategy or field support strategy as opposed to the consultative strategy, you can also have the screener ask questions more specifically attuned to these strategies, such as these:

- "Please describe the level of product knowledge you have, not only of your company's products but also of your competitors' products."

- "To what extent can you provide me with competitive information on products similar to yours?"

- "To the extent that Mr. Smith offers seminars for clients and prospective clients, what tools do you offer—such as well-designed group presentations—that have been particularly effective in working with affluent clients?"

- "Are you available for one-on-one sales presentations to select clients or prospective clients when appropriate?"

The screener can end the call by saying, "Thanks for answering these questions. I'll check with Mr. Smith, consult the calendar and then get back to you." The screener should then prepare a short summary of the call. In some cases, the screener might be very clear that this is not a wholesaler you want to work with, but in most cases you'll need to make the final decision. Sometimes, it will be obvious that the wholesaler has nothing to offer beyond his or her own firm's product information. In most of these cases you will call the wholesaler back and politely decline the meeting, unless the product information being offered is directly on point for your target niche or otherwise fills a critical knowledge gap (such as in our concentrated stock position example above).

Having identified the wholesalers you want to meet with in person, once again it pays to prepare. Before your meeting, create a written agenda and send it in advance by email. Given the screening process, the wholesaler will already be aware that your expectations surpass those of most advisors. Still, by putting forward specific topics of discussion and deliverables, you are more likely to begin to build the consultative coaching relationship you want.

Of course, you must respect the wholesaler's purpose as well and allow him or her to tell you about the company, products and recent enhancements in the context of assisting you in building your wealth management business. Remember that your goal is to forge a business partnership with a select number of top wholesalers who can truly make a difference in your success.

Your screening process and agenda may not be the norm, but it probably won't be a first for the wholesaler. Moreover, good wholesalers will rise to the occasion when they know that they've got a top advisor to potentially work with—someone who knows the difference between a free lunch (or a dozen golf balls) and a real relationship. At the end of the day, the best wholesalers want to work with the most successful advisors. Only the best wholesalers will be able to meet your expectations, and those are the ones you want to work with. Most successful advisors have five or fewer wholesalers whom they regularly see.

Getting the Most from Your Wholesaler Relationships

Even working with the best wholesalers, it's still up to you to get the most value possible from these relationships. The following three actions will help you to optimize each of your wholesaler relationships.

Use Field Support Carefully

Just because a wholesaler offers a service does not always mean that you should use it. For example, while many wholesalers are happy to make seminar presentations for you (or together with you), you should generally forgo this route. Your goal is to build relationships with presentation attendees, making it counterproductive for someone beyond your expert team or strategic alliances to do the talking. Of course, if the wholesaler is a true master at giving presentations, it may make sense to share the stage with him or her a few times in order to enhance your skill set through real-time tutoring and feedback.

As another example, wholesalers may also offer to close cases on your behalf. While this might be tempting, it detracts from your positioning as the advisor who solves the challenges of clients in your niche market.

Industry research shows that this particular lesson is clear to elite advisors. One CEG Worldwide study found that nearly half (46.2 percent) of lower-income advisors want wholesalers in the field who can close cases for them, while only 7.1 percent of higher-income advisors want this type of support.

Provide Feedback

Since wholesalers are one of the most costly advisor support tools available, financial institutions want them to be used effectively. It's up to you to tap into these resources and let your product sponsors know when you get great service and when you do not. Smart financial institutions will be responsive to your feedback.

Focus First on a Small Project

You should focus on one key project first so that all involved parties can win—your practice will grow as you serve your clients well, and the wholesaler will share in your success as you increase your assets under management. Remember that wholesalers act in their own enlightened self-interest. Like top advisors, top wholesalers can work with only a limited number of clients. The best ones choose their advisors carefully based on the level of success they expect those advisors to have.

WATCH THE VIDEO ▶ **Profile in Success: Shashin Shah**
Dallas, Texas
www.cegworldwide.com/btbook/shashin-shah

Outsourcing or Delegating Everything Else

Running your business requires many types of skills apart from pure relationship building and business development. You are often pulled back and forth between back-office problems and client opportunities, with a significant impact on your profitability. You can avoid nearly all these distractions, however, by applying the rule of the four D's to every task, in this order:

1. **Drop it.** If there is no compelling business reason to spend time on a task—either your time or a team member's time—then drop it. When it comes to nonrevenue activities, you can nearly always drop them.

2. **Defer it.** If you are unsure whether a task will result in a positive benefit for your clients or your practice, defer it. Schedule a time to re-evaluate it, and make a decision at that time to drop it, delegate it or do it.

3. **Delegate it.** When a task lies clearly outside of your core competencies, delegate it, either to a staff person or to an outsourcing partner.

4. **Do it.** If a task is part of one of your core competencies and if none of the previous three D's is appropriate, then—and only then—do it.

If you run your business efficiently, you will find that you are able to delegate every function outside of your core competencies. To delegate at this high level, you will almost certainly need to outsource at least some of your business functions.

Preferred Outsourcing Options

As we saw in Chapter 6, using technology wisely frees you from myriad administrative tasks. But technology is only one part of the solution. Finding and managing qualified independent contractors to whom you can outsource a variety of tasks is the other.

There are two preferred options. The first is to outsource everything you can to either your broker-dealer or to your turnkey asset management program (TAMP). This is the best outsourcing alternative.

However, if your financial institution partner cannot meet these needs, you can turn to the second option, which is to outsource specific noncore functions to independent providers on an as-needed basis. This is your classic "make or buy" (or, in this case, "rent") decision.

Determining What You Will Outsource

The first step in successful outsourcing is to identify what you can call on others to do. Your job is to determine which tasks you will do yourself, which you will rely on an institutional partner to do and which you will need independent contractors to do.

As we saw in our discussion on blueprinting systems and processes, you should describe and document every function in your business. Revisit

EXHIBIT 7.1
Services Outsourced by Financial Advisors

Service	Financial Advisors Outsourcing This Service
Web site design	30.1%
Web site maintenance	23.4%
Newsletter	13.9%
Accounting	13.6%
Marketing	12.5%
Technology support	11.3%
Graphic design	11.0%
Portfolio reporting	9.3%
Client surveys	8.3%
Training	6.9%
Bookkeeping	6.8%
Public relations	5.8%
Video production and/or editing	5.1%
Writing	4.2%
Virtual assistant	2.6%
Transcription	2.2%

N = 2,108 financial advisors. Source: CEG Worldwide, 2012.

your blueprints to help identify the specific tasks that would be more effectively or profitably completed by an outsourcing partner than by an in-house team member.

Our 2012 survey found that financial advisors are outsourcing a wide array of tasks, as shown in **Exhibit 7.1**.

Outsourcing to Independent Contractors

More and more advisors are turning to independent contractors—freelancers—to fill many of their non-client relationship tasks and, as a result, are enjoying higher profit margins and better quality control. They are finding that such independent contractors are often much more focused and committed to successfully completing projects than are employees.

Even though independent contractors do offer many advantages, they also present a new set of challenges when it comes to finding, hiring and managing them. We recommend undertaking the following three stages and the specific actions within each stage to make your outsourcing as successful as possible.

Stage 1: Planning

1. **Define your needs.** Decide exactly what you will outsource. Pull together your current costs of doing each function in-house. Be clear on the results you hope to achieve by outsourcing (such as lower costs, improved performance, enhanced service or overall responsiveness). If it's a large outsourcing project, design a request for proposal (RFP) that includes performance metrics, evaluation criteria, a scoring process, and a financial model to evaluate price or cost.

2. **Define the needed skills.** Determine the specific skills that you need in an independent contractor before you start searching for one. Most

individuals specialize, so don't expect to find a broad range of diverse skills in any one person (and if you do, expect to pay very well for it).

3. **Anticipate issues.** Take a moment to think through the effect on your business of outsourcing this particular function. If necessary, act to head off any potential issues or problems.

Stage 2: Selection

4. **Obtain referrals.** Because more and more advisors are moving toward virtual offices, they can be your best source of referrals for high-quality independent contractors with experience in the financial services industry.

5. **Interview candidates.** Identify the most qualified candidates and interview them. Again, if it's a large project, evaluate the candidates' proposals in response to your RFP.

6. **Check references.** Once you identify a good candidate, always ask for references. Check each of those references, and make sure to ask if they know whom else that independent contractor is working with—and place a call to those firms as well. Often you will get a very different and much more insightful perspective because these additional references will not have been preselected by the independent contractor.

7. **Create a good fit with existing team.** Independent contractors should complement your existing team by bringing in new expertise and talent. They should not displace or alienate your team by being brought in for interesting projects that your current staff is perfectly capable of doing a good job with. Simply duplicating existing skills will only erode the morale of your permanent team and gain you little. Where appropriate, involve your staff in independent contractor hiring decisions.

8. **Select your new provider.** When choosing among two or three finalists, be sure to weigh the relationship factor in your final selection. Expertise is key, but so are credibility and chemistry.

Stage 3: Implementation

9. **Negotiate the written contract.** Once you have selected the leading candidate, negotiate the details of your contract. Create a clear agreement that defines the project, deliverables, deadlines and benchmarks. It should spell out the billing and payment process and deal with any intellectual property issues and noncompete provisions. An employment attorney can draft a boilerplate agreement that you can use over and over.

10. **Start slowly.** As you begin working with an independent contractor, start with bite-size pieces. Assign a meaningful project (but not one that is mission-critical) for which you might pay in the low four figures, to assess the contractor's performance. If you are forced to outsource a mission-critical project to an unfamiliar contractor, you can evaluate the contractor on the fly much as you would a potential employee. Hire the contractor as a consultant to put together a plan for how he or she would complete the project in the assigned time frame. Have the person talk to clients and internal staff as appropriate and then present his or her solution to you.

11. **Manage and monitor.** Be clear about expectations, but don't micromanage. Let freelancers be freelancers, and allow them to freely use their own expertise and creativity to achieve high-quality results. Give them access to internal staff and resources as needed. Set up a clear channel of communication, preferably with a single point person in your firm, so that you can be apprised of project progress and so that your independent contractors can keep current with any changes in the firm that affect projects. Give them every opportunity to succeed.

12. **Pay promptly.** We all appreciate being paid promptly. If independent contractors are diligent about completing their projects in a timely manner, they will be justifiably irked if you then take too much time to process their invoices. And you will quickly get a reputation as a slow payer among the network of freelancers, making it more difficult for you to bring on good talent.

A Checklist for Conscious Partnering

Whether you are considering working with a financial institution, wholesaler or independent contractor, evaluate and choose each one deliberately and systematically. Ask yourself these questions:

The last item on this checklist points to the need to make good, proactive, business-building choices on an ongoing basis. You may download a

---

Conscious Partnering Checklist

❏ Am I effectively outsourcing everything that I can—and should—so that I can focus on my core competencies?

❏ Given my chosen clientele and market niche, do I have the right number and quality of external relationships in place?

❏ Am I deep-down satisfied with the financial institutions that I rely upon for critical services such as custody of clients' funds and the products and services that I offer?

❏ Have I created a system for screening the wholesalers I want to work with? Do I use it effectively?

❏ Am I making the most effective and most efficient use of each of my external relationships, whether with a financial institution, a wholesaler, or a third-party service or product provider?

❏ Do I have a good system in place for identifying, hiring, managing and paying independent contractors?

❏ Have I made it a priority to regularly (at least annually) review all my external relationships?

© Copyright 2013 CEG Worldwide, LLC.

PDF of this checklist at http://www.cegworldwide.com/downloads/bt-book/eb_ceg_conscious_partnering_checklist.pdf. Even if you have been diligent, whatever you know (or think you know) right now is unlikely to include everything that you will actually need to know in six months or a year. To succeed as an entrepreneurial advisor to the affluent, you need to commit to lifelong (or at least career-long) learning, which we turn to in the next chapter.

Chapter 8
Commit to Lifelong Learning

To become an elite financial advisor in our rapidly evolving industry, you must commit to lifelong learning. It's as simple as that. Not only will your clients expect you to stay abreast of important developments, but today's regulatory environment demands that you stay up-to-date. And you obviously want to give yourself every possible advantage as you grow your business. Ongoing learning will give you this edge.

We suggest that you focus on two distinct areas of learning:

- **Practice management issues.** What are the best practices of top financial advisors? How can you implement these practices in your own business? What's new and valuable that you shouldn't miss? How can you more effectively move upmarket? What critical new research must you know about?

- **Strategic wealth management knowledge.** With regard to everything from asset allocation and portfolio construction to tax management strategies and legal developments, it's important to keep current on the state of the art in wealth management. You are looking here not so much for in-depth knowledge of advanced planning areas as a high-level overview of sophisticated concepts in order to flag your clients' issues and leverage the right experts to provide optimal solutions.

We recommend two very different types of activities to address these two areas. The first is to work with a mentor, coach or consultant. The second is to create a formal learning program for yourself and your team. We will specifically describe how to go about these activities, but keep in mind these general steps:

- **Conduct a self-review:** Start with a frank assessment of where you and your staff are now and where there are gaps in your knowledge and skills. Which educational activities would fill in these gaps so you can deliver even better service and solutions to your clients?

- **Be steady and consistent:** Lifelong learning is not a sprint but a never-ending journey toward an ever-growing summit of knowledge. Take your time, engage in the learning process in the most effective ways you can (this is not an area where you can afford to cut costs) and remember to enjoy yourself along the way.

- **Pay attention to the knowing-doing gap:** As we discussed in Chapter 2, the knowing-doing gap presents a pervasive challenge for all of us. Knowledge by itself won't do you any good; you have to know how to use it well. Unfortunately, many corporate-style training programs dispense a great deal of intellectual knowledge but offer little in the way of actual application. When you go back to the office and try to employ what you have learned, you often find that things are very different than in the training course and that implementing effective and lasting change takes more than just knowing how to do something.

WATCH THE VIDEO ▶ **Profile in Success: Mike Pazera**
Rockport, Texas
www.cegworldwide.com/btbook/mike-pazera

Working with a Mentor, Coach or Consultant

A good mentor, coach or consultant will help you create a vision of what you want your life and practice to be and then help you achieve it. This individual will enable you to start thinking of your time horizon as many years, not just a few months. Just as elite athletes have coaches who help ensure their best performances, a coach, mentor or consultant can be a true partner who holds you accountable for living up to your full potential.

Even more, a good coach, mentor or consultant can help you fill in the gaps in your competencies; keep up with developments in your area of expertise; and apply your new knowledge, in real time, in your specific business environment, thus helping you to surmount the knowing-doing gap. An effective mentor, coach or consultant—someone who can provide both knowledge and a formal "learning and doing" structure to support what you want to achieve—can therefore play a vital role in your efforts to build a world-class wealth management business.

Six Steps to Leveraging Mentors, Coaches and Consultants

To optimize your relationship with a coach, mentor or consultant, we highly recommend the following six steps:

Step 1. Perform a Self-Assessment

Before anything else, sit down and have a serious conversation with yourself. Ask yourself: What is it that you *really* want? Imagine yourself in the future: What do you want your life to look like in one year? Five years? Twenty years? Don't limit yourself to what you want to achieve in business, but look at the entire picture, including your family life, your leisure time and your health. Remember we are in business to build the quality of life we want. Compare where you are now to where you want to go. What do you need to get there? What are your major concerns?

Make this a serious self-assessment and be as objective as you possibly can. It will help to look at yourself as your spouse or a close friend might see you. The willingness to perform this kind of candid self-assessment is a clear indication that you have the commitment that a good coach or mentor will require.

Step 2. Define Your Areas of Focus

Using your self-assessment, and looking back at Chapter 6's work on creating a compelling vision and business plan, define the specific areas where you want to change or improve over the next 12 months. For example, you might want to work with affluent clients who each have at least $2 million in investable assets. In addition, you may want to implement systems that will elevate your client service in order to increase your assets under management and net profit by a certain percentage. You might also include areas from your personal life that you identified in your self-assessment.

Step 3. Choose Between a Mentor, a Coach or a Consultant

Once you have a clear idea of what you'd like to achieve, you'll be in a position to ask: Who might help me with these particular issues? Who can offer me optimal assistance? Mentors, coaches and consultants each bring unique qualities to the table.

Mentors are ideal to work with because the right one will have already attained the level of success that you want to achieve and will help you realize the same or even greater success. The best mentor will already be a leading advisor, will have already traveled the road you are now traveling, and will have great experiences and in-depth knowledge that he or she is willing to share with you.

Unfortunately, there are just not that many mentors available in our industry. Many financial institutions and some trade associations try to foster mentoring, but it is usually designed for advisors just getting started or for those in the midmarket. At the high end of the market, finding a mentor really comes down to personal relationships. If you know and like someone who has already achieved substantial success, then you should definitely consider asking him or her to be your mentor. Mentors are typically not compensated at all or at most receive nominal compensation.

Still, you will want to establish some type of formal relationship where you get together in person or speak on the phone on a regular basis.

However, unless you are very lucky or very gifted in developing relationships (or both), you are unlikely to have access to a true mentor other than for short periods during your career. Instead, you probably need to engage either a coach or a consultant.

Coaches may or may not have expertise in the financial world. Instead, they are experts in helping you identify what you want, creating a plan to achieve your goals, and enabling you to keep your energy and focus sustained over time to arrive at your destination. As with a mentor, a coach will work with you on a long-term basis. Because coaches typically work over the phone, you will have no geographic restrictions. In our experience, if you work with a competent coach, especially one with expertise in financial services, you should expect to see at least a 25 percent growth in both your net income and assets under management in the first 12 months.

To find out more about how coaching can help you achieve your specific goals, download CEG Worldwide's free white paper, *The Right Coach: A Guide for Financial Advisors*

Consultants are typically brought in for the short term to solve a specific challenge. These challenges usually revolve around strategy, marketing and other big-picture items that you need to address before you can move forward. These might include your firm's structure or strategic positioning, a merger or acquisition, or your technology system. Consultants have expertise in areas that you do not and can thus add greatly to your skill set, particularly in areas that are beyond your core competencies. Because consultants work with you over a defined period on one or more specific challenges, the nature of your relationship with a consultant will be fundamentally different than with a mentor or coach.

Step 4. Choose the Right Individual

Once you have decided whether a mentor, coach or consultant is most appropriate for your situation, take these four actions to locate and evaluate candidates:

1. **Identify candidates.** Whom do you most admire in the field where you wish to excel? Who is enjoying the most success? Many successful advisors have coaches, mentors or consultants and can offer you referrals.

2. **Get in touch.** Ask the candidate how he or she was able to succeed. You want to find out not just what the individual knows, but also whether he or she is someone you can learn from. He or she should be able to engage you in a way that connects with you and touches on your ambitions. Someone may be a top expert in the field, but if you don't feel a personal connection, that person is not right for you.

3. **Interview.** Meet with each candidate to find out whether his or her skill set meets your needs and your personalities mesh. Ask about his or her background and specifically about having worked with someone in your situation with goals similar to your own. Because it's easier to understand an approach by actually experiencing it—rather than just describing it—many coaches, mentors and consultants will offer you a free practice coaching session.

4. **Ask.** If you feel that a particular person might be a good coach or mentor, ask whether he or she would be willing to work with you in your area. If the individual is not a good match, ask for a referral to someone who might be.

If you are searching for a **coach** or **mentor**, keep these things in mind as you talk to candidates:

- **The relationship is key.** You, not the coach or mentor, should always be the center of attention. You should feel powerful in this context and feel recharged after each session. This will help you sustain your momentum between meetings.

- **You should feel safe and courageous with your coach or mentor.** Be open to exploring new ideas and opportunities that you would normally avoid. You must be willing to take risks with this person. Only when you take risks will new opportunities open for you.

- **The relationship must be confidential.** You should never have to worry about sharing information with your coach or mentor.

- **There must be trust on both sides.** You must believe that the coach or mentor is truly on your side and believes that you will do what you say you will do.

- **There must be honesty.** The coaching or mentoring relationship must be one in which you are able to tell the whole truth about yourself without concern about looking good or being judged. You should also expect that your coach or mentor will speak the unvarnished truth about you as he or she sees it. The relationship is not about being nice. It's about being direct and effective.

- **The coach or mentor should be able to make bold requests yet not be attached to outcomes.** The outcomes are yours. The coach or mentor is there to help you achieve the ones you choose.

On the other hand, if you have decided to work with a **consultant**, look for someone who has demonstrated success in working with firms like yours. Note that just like top advisors, the best consultants get their business through relationship marketing, especially referrals from your peers, financial institutions and strategic allies. Finally, don't work with a consultant who does not have industry-specific experience—you'll end up paying that person to learn the business on your time.

Step 5. Make an Agreement and Action Plan

Your goal is to close the gap between what you have and what you want. Most coaches, mentors and consultants will want to work within the framework of a very clear agreement about the results you want to achieve within a specified time frame. This agreement will precisely define your ambitions—what you are truly passionate about and are willing, even eager, to work hard to achieve.

We often get caught up in things that we think we ought to be doing, usually as defined by someone else. Simply wanting something because it sounds like something we *should* want is not enough. A skilled individual will help you get in touch with your real ambitions and will do so in a nonjudgmental way.

You should also create a detailed action plan that will identify the steps you will take and the barriers you might encounter. Your coach, mentor or consultant will gauge how much confidence you have in actually accomplishing each step and will help you craft a realistic plan.

Step 6. Work Your Plan

Many coaches, mentors and consultants will want you to make a minimum commitment—typically six months to a year—in which some real work can get done. During this assessment period, examine your progress. Are you making the improvements you want? Do you have the ambition to move forward, or are you feeling pushed along? Are you enthusiastic about continuing the process, or do you feel resistance? Assuming that the process is working for you, move ahead.

When you bump into barriers on the path, a coach, mentor or consultant will help you see the difference between obstacles that are actually outside of you and those that are within you. This will help get you around barriers that otherwise might have stopped your progress. If you don't meet your goals, he or she will help you learn from this and determine what you can do differently.

A good coach, mentor or consultant will also help reveal things to you about yourself that you may never have noticed. By uncovering these blind spots, you will be able to make choices and see opportunities that you previously might have missed. Perhaps most valuable of all, this person can help you start to understand that your ambitions are larger—and more attainable—than you ever thought.

> **WATCH THE VIDEO** ▶ **Get with the Learning Program**
> With John Bowen
> www.cegworldwide.com/btbook/get-with-the-program

Establish a Formal Learning Program

In addition to working with a coach, mentor or consultant, we urge you to establish a formal learning program for both you and your staff. Such a program will keep you and your staff up-to-date on changing markets and client needs as well as on evolving products and services.

Many types of learning programs are readily available, including these:

- **Programs provided by financial institutions.** As we discussed in Chapter 7, aim to take advantage of the financial institutions that offer you and your staff substantial support and training.

- **Designations offered by industry associations.** Depending on your goals, it may be appropriate for you and/or senior members of your staff to pursue some of the worthwhile designations, including, but not limited to, Certified Financial Planner (CFP), Chartered Financial Analyst (CFA) and Certified Investment Management Analyst (CIMA).

- **Learning programs presented by industry organizations.** Many industry professional associations, including the Financial Planning

Association, the National Association of Fee-Only Planners and the Investment Management Consultants Association, convene annual national and regional conferences, as well as offer e-learning programs, covering specific areas or expertise.

Six Steps to an Effective Learning Program

Your learning program should be well-planned and formalized. A hit-and-miss approach will yield hit-and-miss results—something you can't afford. Since your staff is integral to your efforts, include them in your program. And importantly, with respect to spending time and money on ongoing learning, don't be "penny-wise and pound-foolish." Wise investments in training and learning are essential to your long-term success in building a world-class business.

We suggest the following six steps to establish an effective learning program:

Step 1. Identify Areas for Development and Areas of Strength

Given the costs of training—in both time and money—you want to focus on precisely those issues that will provide the greatest results. Consider any weak links and areas that could benefit from special attention, especially gaps in skills relevant to delivering a superlative client experience. Where do people need help in addressing challenges? Also, who shines at particular tasks? Would it be worthwhile to enhance these strengths even further?

Step 2. Identify Specific Areas of Focus

Examine each area to determine the specific skills, knowledge or experience that you or your staff must acquire in order to address those areas. For example, as your firm's or team's rainmaker, you may need to take a public speaking class or work with a consultant who specializes in highly effective presentations. Or if you have a staff member struggling with a particular technology tool, a one-day class could solve the problem.

Step 3. Identify Specific Learning Events

Once you have identified the specific areas where both you and individual staff members will focus, determine the particular events, classes or groups that you or your staff members will attend or take part in. Because any program will take valuable time away from your business, be sure to establish in advance whether it has a high likelihood of delivering the learning experience you need. Spend a few minutes on the phone with program providers to find out exactly what they offer. Ask for references of other advisors (or their staff members) who have taken part in the same program. If the expertise or tools aren't exactly what you need—if they are unlikely to add real value—then politely decline.

Step 4. Map Out the Learning Program

Chart out your learning activities for the next 12 months. Post the chart in your office so that everyone is clear on which issues are being addressed, how and when. Enter the activities on your electronic intra-office calendar if you have one.

Step 5. Take Part in All Learning Activities

Make your attendance and that of your staff a top priority at every scheduled learning opportunity. Set an example by meticulously monitoring your own attendance and participation, and make sure your staff knows that you expect their best efforts as well.

Step 6. Apply What You Have Learned

Systematically integrate new knowledge into the services you offer to your clients. Having spent the time and money needed to acquire this knowledge, make sure that you leverage it to add maximum value to your business.

In fact, as an entrepreneurial advisor, maximizing your business's value in order to create equity is something you always want to keep your eye on and is the subject we'll turn to next.

Chapter 9
Build Maximum Equity

THROUGHOUT THIS BOOK WE'VE ASKED YOU TO THINK LIKE an entrepreneur and to treat your practice as a business. This will enable you to build a simple and elegant wealth management business that is a joy to run and that delights your clients. By consistently focusing on building maximum equity, you will also create an extremely valuable business.

We've saved this seventh strategy—build maximum equity in your business—for the end because we wanted you to first understand how to create a great business that not only would serve fewer, wealthier clients, but would give you the lifestyle you want. (Remember when we urged you to read straight through the book before trying to apply anything? This is the point we wanted you to get to.) Now that you know how to build a great business, we want you to keep your eye on one more thing: building your business to ensure its maximum value.

It may surprise you to learn that the "CEG" in "CEG Worldwide" stands for "Creating Equity Group." As an organization, we embrace equity creation as part of our mission because we've seen far too many advisors at the ends of their careers who have not achieved their dreams. Consider how you were recruited into the industry. Recruiters tell prospective advisors that their greatest challenge will be to decide just how much money they want to make and how soon. With just a little hard work, they say, you can achieve the American dream. Unfortunately, many advisors have realized only one part of that dream—the hard work.

Think about why you got into the business in the first place. Part of the motivation for many of us was to help solve clients' financial challenges. Having a positive impact on a significant number of successful families is a real accomplishment to be proud of. But while a client-centered focus is important, you must also build your business to support the quality of life you want for your own family as well—if you're not able to take care of your family, then you probably won't be able to do a good job for your clients.

Your clients feel the same way. They want to work with someone who has the self-respect and wisdom to keep his or her own financial house in order. They know that you can't take care of them if you can't even take care of yourself.

So making sure your financial stake in your business is as great as possible makes sense from all perspectives. Your challenge is to focus on building a practice that the marketplace will value highly.

It's never too early to take the steps necessary to build substantial equity in your business. This is true whether you are a sole practitioner or work smack-dab in the middle of a major firm. In fact, as with investing for retirement, the sooner you start making an ongoing investment in equity creation, the better your position will be later on when it comes time to sell or otherwise transition out of your business.

Benefits for Everyone

Thinking like an entrepreneur in order to build a valuable business is both farsighted and completely appropriate regardless of where you happen to work. It doesn't matter if you are employed by a wirehouse, are an independent broker-dealer representative inside a large office or are a registered investment advisor with your own firm. Regardless of your specific situation, building equity will pay huge dividends.

By staying focused on building equity, you will personally be better off, both now and in the long run. Think about the last time you sold a home. In order to make it show well, you very likely spruced it up and made all those minor repairs you'd been putting off. As a result, it never looked or felt better. Similarly, even if you aren't looking to exit your business any time soon, really "taking care of business" now will markedly increase both your cash flow and your enjoyment of your business.

Similarly, as we've shown throughout this book, your clients will be better off because they'll get the attention and world-class service that they want and expect. So a big part of creating a business that is as valuable as possible comes from providing the very consultative client relationship management process and top-notch service that most satisfies your wealthy clients. This puts you and your clients in the same boat, being lifted by the same entrepreneurial tide. The result is a "no brainer," a win-win for everyone. This makes our first and last strategies—attract wealthy clients and build maximum equity—a mirror image of one another: The very things you do to attract and then retain wealthy clients are also the things that will build tremendous value.

Finally, whether you are in a position to actually sell your business or work in a firm where you can take advantage of increasingly attractive sunset provisions, everyone comes out a winner. When you sell your business to another advisor or firm, clearly they see the value in it and are happy to take over, for a reasonable price that benefits you both, what you have created. And in fact, in recent years we've seen an active and growing marketplace as advisory businesses have evolved and some of the individuals running them have reached traditional retirement age.

If you are employed by a wirehouse, the equation changes slightly, but everyone involved nonetheless will end up benefiting from your entrepreneurial equity-maximizing approach. Because today's firms realize the importance of succession planning and the advantages of incenting their advisors to create as much value as possible, almost all firms now offer sunset provisions that will enable you to tiptoe out of the business over three to five years. And note that while independent advisors have more flexibility in selling their businesses outright, wirehouse advisors have two competitive advantages. They can leverage their firms' brands, and they have guaranteed "buyers" standing by who are ready to finance the transactions.

A typical sunset provision will give you in excess of two times revenue over three to five years, and you'll know the check on the back end is as good as your relationships are now with your existing clients. If you have built a valuable business and your clients stay on with the successor advisor, you will do very well. If your successor advisor can grow the business even more, you will do even better. But it all begins with the foundation you leave and the real value that you have built up in your business over time. Obviously, the firms themselves also benefit when advisors follow a value-driven entrepreneurial approach, because such advisors create a much more valuable set of client relationships and business processes that remain for the long term.

The Four C's of Creating Equity

You can tell whether you're on the road to maximizing the value of your business by objectively assessing the four C's of creating equity. These are the four primary drivers of value in a financial advisory business that will cause buyers (or successor advisors in a big firm) to covet what you've created:

1. Cash flow
2. Clients
3. Company
4. Competitors

1. Cash Flow

The single most important thing you can do to create equity is to maximize your cash flow and profit margins. Every buyer of a business (and every advisor who "buys" a business through a sunset provision transition) takes into account the discounted value of current cash flow. The more cash flow you have, and especially the more your cash flow is growing and the higher your profit margins, the more value you will have demonstrated. In the best of all worlds, your cash flow will continue to grow and your margins will continue to expand in a straight upward-sloping line. An up-and-down or bumpy line is clearly less desirable.

As you consider cash flow, don't mistake it for good revenues. While obviously you can't have a lot of cash flow and good margins without great revenues, cash flow is still the byproduct of good margins. Revenues, on the other hand, are the byproduct of good growth. Financial advisory businesses can generate substantial profit margins at every size, so make sure that you are matching up your costs with your revenues from the get-go.

2. Clients

You want your clients to have a demonstrable pattern of high retention and high satisfaction, a strong tendency to provide introductions, and a predisposition to not be tied to a single person at your firm (even you). Smart potential buyers will spend a good deal of time looking at your clients. To the extent that your clients all enjoy the same simple and elegant experience of your consultative process, it will be easier for you to demonstrate a high level of satisfaction and ongoing loyalty through a formal process, such as a client survey.

3. Company

You should be able to show high retention and satisfaction of employees or team members, both in terms of their work environment and their compensation. Be prepared to tell success stories of employees or team members who have moved up through the ranks, taken on additional responsibility and grown their compensation along the way.

You also need to be able to demonstrate good business management in these areas:

- Financial management and processes
- Client management and processes
- Employee (or team) management and processes
- Operations management and processes

4. Competitors

You want a business model that competitors either cannot figure out or that is difficult to replicate. Your competitors should be in awe of your business model's growth and profitability. However, don't think that this means that you have to have some sort of complicated trade secret that drives your success. In fact, what competitors are most often in awe of is an extremely simple business that works extremely well.

In this book we've laid out the wealth management business model and shown you how to make it work. Incredibly, as our research has found, only 6.6 percent of surveyed advisors with more than $50 million in assets under management are using this model. This gives you every opportunity to differentiate yourself and leave your competitors in awe of the growth and profitability of your business model. If your business is working so well that your competitors either want to join with you or acquire you, you will know you are on the right track.

> **WATCH THE VIDEO** ▶ **The Off Ramp**
> With John Bowen
> www.cegworldwide.com/btbook/the-off-ramp

Organic vs. Alternative Growth

You can follow one of two approaches to creating value and equity in your business over time. The first is organic growth, or building a great business by serving your clients well over time. Pursuing organic growth has real advantages. You get to keep control over everything, from the direction of your business and the way it's managed to the number and depth of your client relationships.

The other approach, alternative growth, accelerates growth through acquiring, merging with or partnering with another advisory business. Unfortunately, many studies have indicated that the failure rate among mergers is roughly 70 percent, so be very careful about taking an alternative approach when the organic methods we recommend are so reliably successful.

Given the nature of how capital works and grows, any advisor worth his or her salt will experience a reasonable amount of organic growth. But by using the wealth management model and the strategies we describe in this book, your organic growth will look a lot like the alternative growth that other advisors can get only by buying or selling a business, which, as we just stated, can be fraught with uncertainty and unexpected difficulties. As a great entrepreneur who pursues organic growth to build a simple and elegant business, you'll probably be a lot happier. (And if you need help implementing our strategies, you can benefit from the mentoring, coaching or consulting we described in the last chapter.)

Certainly, before you pursue any alternative growth strategy, make sure your business is completely in order, with all equity-maximizing systems in place. If you are in a position to sell your business outright, this will provide you with the highest valuation and the best opportunity to prevent a cultural mismatch that could cause failure. In addition, if you are considering a deal of any type, bring in an outside expert who really knows how to maximize the price you get for your business or to minimize what you have to pay for someone else's. Especially in the case of selling your business, you'll probably only do it once in a lifetime, so if there were ever a time to bring in a true professional, this would be it.

Of course, there's already one true professional in the picture: you. And for the benefit of that true professional, we'll now turn to our final chapter, where we will provide a framework for transforming the vision we have given you in this book into the reality of your everyday experience.

Chapter 10
Making It Real

I T'S REMARKABLE HOW WELL YOU CAN DO FOR YOURSELF while doing well for others. The impact you can have on your clients by aligning their financial assets to support their most important values and goals is simply tremendous. Collectively, as financial advisors, we really do have an unbelievable opportunity to change the world in positive ways. At the same time, we can get paid very well and also have an outstanding quality of life. That's about as good as it gets.

Is it easy to make this happen? Frankly, no, it's not, especially at first, and even more so if you are trying to do it all on your own. That's why we wrote this book: to present a direct, no-nonsense road map to success. It's also why we provide the coaching programs described later. If your mission is to build a top-tier wealth management business that makes the world a better place for you and your clients, we want to help you.

The Big Picture

Let's take a step back and take a look at the big picture. If you have read this far, you are likely motivated to make the changes in your practice that will dramatically elevate the level of service you provide to your clients while taking you far toward achieving your breakthrough goals.

So what do you do next? How can you actually implement our recommendations? What do you need to do to make it all real?

First, we suggest that you commit these four maxims to memory:

1. **Be successful on purpose.** As we have stressed throughout this book, success demands intentional action. When you begin with the end in mind and commit to the necessary hard work and planning, your odds of success rise dramatically.

2. **Think like an entrepreneur.** Whether you are independent or employed by a big firm, you're in business for yourself. This means that to be extremely successful, you have to think like an entrepreneur who has chosen to be in the wealth management business.

3. **Work with fewer, wealthier clients.** If you are determined to be successful on purpose and are thinking like an entrepreneur, your single best course of action is to identify a niche of wealthy individuals and provide them with the world-class service and consultative wealth management that will delight them and motivate them to provide both additional assets and qualified referrals.

4. **Outsource what you can (and should).** If you attempt to build a highly successful wealth management business on your own, you will fail to reach your full potential. Determine where you add the most value—which in most cases will be client relationship management, expert relationship management and business development—and outsource the rest. Don't try to go it on your own.

Second, review the seven strategies we've presented. The overview in Chapter 1 is a good place to start. With the big picture in mind, it will be much easier to create the road map you need to navigate from where you are now to where you want to be in the not-too-distant future.

Third, commit to overcoming the knowing-doing gap that we described in Chapter 2. In accordance with the "Outsource what you can" maxim, you may find that you need some help to bridge the knowing-doing gap.

Ironically, when we founded CEG Worldwide, we thought it would be sufficient to provide financial advisors with research and training in best practices. But having been through the entrepreneurial fire many times ourselves, we should have realized that knowledge alone isn't enough. Most people, including most advisors, need help in implementing what they learn. Whether you choose us or someone else, we believe that working with a qualified coach, mentor or consultant will dramatically accelerate your efforts to build a successful wealth management business.

The Power of Planning

There's little doubt that virtually every financial advisor is in business to succeed, to enjoy a good income, to serve clients well and to have a great lifestyle. But some advisors are extremely successful, while many others are just hanging on. What's the difference between them?

In our experience, it isn't talent—we've known plenty of incredibly smart, talented advisors who never seem to achieve the level of success they deserve. Nor is it opportunity. We've known advisors who were presented with great opportunities that they never managed to turn into real success.

So what's the key? We believe it's being focused and ready for change. The top advisors envision their success, draw up clear plans for getting there and then find effective ways to incorporate the needed changes into their practices.

Our experience with hundreds of elite financial advisors tells us that they consistently take these actions:

- They formulate a vision of what their lives will be like in the next three years.

- They clearly define the goals needed to realize their vision and then commit to achieving them.

- They identify the strategies and tactics they will need to implement to achieve their goals, with particular attention paid to planning for early wins.

- They execute their strategies and tactics so as to realize their goals and make sure to celebrate wins along the way.

- They and their coaches regularly review their goals so they can stay focused on what's important in their lives.

- They hold themselves accountable for breaking through into higher levels of success.

Top financial advisors understand that once they have an intention to succeed, many of their perceived obstacles will disappear. That is, they intentionally position themselves to achieve success. They understand in their bones that the popular cliché "Where there's a will, there's a way" is quite true.

To maximize the probability that you will succeed, be clear about your intentions for success. Successful people do what unsuccessful people are not willing to do. In today's marketplace, you have a great opportunity for success—again, despite the fact that more and more advisors are calling themselves wealth managers, there are actually fewer true wealth managers today than there were several years ago—but you must be proactive. We strongly recommend that you purposefully design your own future by creating a road map—a plan—of the steps ahead.

Don't put yourself at a disadvantage by failing to develop a plan. Without one, it's easy to become overwhelmed by the challenges you face. But a plan that incorporates the goals that you are passionate about achieving will keep you focused on your priorities and on track until you manifest your vision.

Get Started

With your vision and goals clearly defined, and with an intelligent and realistic plan set forth, your next—and far more challenging—step is to take the actions that will achieve your goals.

Successful change is a real challenge in part because typically no one else—team members, partners or management—reacts well to change except the person who is driving it. When change comes, we all tend to immediately put our hands up and try to figure out how to avoid it. Behaviorists tell us that 80 percent of us are reactive thinkers who will do anything to avoid change. The other 20 percent are creative thinkers, meaning we initially try to avoid the change but then examine and judge whether it's good or bad change. If we think it's a good change, we will incorporate it into our lives. When creative thinkers believe it's a change for the worse, they will figure out ways to get around it.

Even with a road map and a serious commitment, you will face substantial challenges. But that's a good thing. To overcome the obstacles that separate winners from losers, you will be called upon to add substantial value. If it were easy to become a world-class wealth manager, everyone would be doing it.

So when you find yourself butting heads or hearts with management or your team members and you just want to quit—don't. If you are clear about the success you want, have put together a workable plan and are willing to do what it takes to succeed, then surely you will.

So commit yourself to the success you want, create a plan to get there and then begin to turn your dreams into reality. The possibilities that we have described in this book are very real and well within your reach. The strategies we have described are the best ones out there. So if that's what you want, get started—right now. We know you can do it, and we wish you the very best of success. Your clients and future clients are counting on you.

John J. Bowen Jr.

Paul Brunswick

Jonathan Powell

About the Authors

John J. Bowen Jr.

CEG Worldwide's founder and CEO, John Bowen has long been known as a leader in the area of adding value to financial services firms. Bowen started his career as an independent broker-dealer representative and then became a fee-based financial advisor. He was ultimately named the CEO of Reinhardt Werba Bowen (RWB), a money management firm that helped other financial advisors raise billions of dollars in assets. In 1998, Bowen became CEO of Assante Capital Management upon the acquisition of RWB by Assante. He left Assante to start CEG Worldwide in 2000 in order to help advisors realize substantial success through the use of CEG Worldwide's business development systems.

He writes a highly acclaimed monthly column for one of the leading financial services trade journals in the United States, *Financial Planning*. He is the author of several books, including *The Prudent Investor's Guide to Beating the Market* and *Creating Equity: How to Build a Hugely Successful Asset Management Business*.

Paul Brunswick

Paul Brunswick brings proven sales, coaching and leadership skills to the CEG Worldwide team. He has extensive financial services experience and a proven track record working with both institutional and ultra-high-net-worth clients, as well as with financial advisors and branch managers. Brunswick has both field and corporate expertise in developing talent at all levels within a financial services organization.

Brunswick has had more than 25 years of success in the financial services industry. Most recently, he was the director of national business development for Smith Barney, where he provided strategic and tactical direction to the firm's entire private client distribution channel. He led campaigns designed to increase advisor net asset flow, grow fee-based revenue, and improve advisor competency in such key areas as investment and wealth management. He also had responsibility for internal communications, new product approval and the research strategy group.

Earlier, he worked at Smith Barney in a variety of management positions across the country. He started his financial career as a financial consultant for Merrill Lynch in St. Louis, Missouri.

Jonathan Powell

Jonathan Powell's expertise in developing top-performing financial advisors is a great asset to the clients he serves through CEG Worldwide. Working with many of the nation's top financial firms, he enjoys helping financial advisors transform their professional and personal lives by implementing CEG Worldwide's research-backed principles.

Powell has hired and coached hundreds of the industry's top financial advisors—in multiple distribution channels—for more than 25 years. After starting his career as an independent financial planner in the San Francisco Bay Area, he went on to spend more than two decades with Citigroup before deciding to pursue his passion for training and coaching.

In his lengthy career, Powell has managed branches for Smith Barney and led Citibank's West Coast brokerage business, overseeing 290 financial advisors and 20 managers. During his branch leadership career he worked side by side with 45 financial advisors, each producing over $1 million of revenue, to help them grow their practices.

Made in the USA
Columbia, SC
23 October 2020